S0-BHW-901

Ranger
(Volume I)

Theodore Enslin

NORTH ATLANTIC BOOKS

Ranger (Volume I)

Copyright © 1978 by Theodore Enslin
0-913028-51-7 - Soft cover
0-913028-58-4 - Hard cover edition (50 copies, signed and numbered)

Publisher's Address (1978 only):

North Atlantic Books
635 Amador Street
Richmond, California 94805

Alternative Forwarding Address:

North Atlantic Books
c/o Richard Grossinger
Grossinger, New York 12734

Principal Distributor for Resale:

Book People
2940 Seventh Street
Berkeley, California 94710

Special thanks are due to Io, Active Anthology (Sumac Press) and Wch Way, in which extended portions first appeared, and to Longhouse and Primer where several other sections may be found.

This project is partially supported by a grant from the National Endowment for the Arts in Washington, D.C., a Federal agency.

This book was set in 10 point Caledonia by Barrett Watten at the West Coast Print Center, Inc., Berkeley, California.

Cover: Lucy Baker

For Alison, who had first news of the Ranger on the
Great Beach at Cape Cod, July 15, 1971

for those who range,

for those at home whose range I see,

but cannot know—

Book I

I

What the man knows of history—
how he will move
through it,
pants down. How he
ranges
       lean wolf
to feed on prey—only
enough for himself
                          and his children—
to suffice.
              His fill.

I sit
       looking across this room.
As always, the pile of letters
to go out on the morning's mail.
(Do they know how much time
it costs me to answer?
The energy and strength?
I sometimes think I work as hard
as any man digging his grave
with a literal shovel—
cut the boards for a coffin,
                          too.)

But to begin it.
                 It is history.
HIS STORY someone said,
partly told,
              mostly obscure.
What truck we have with it.
Truckle or knuckle
                    under.
It is this time in the morning:
11:23,
           and I begin it
(nearly a year late)
but no one need know that—
late, only if I think so.
I do, or I don't.
Moving in to the clinches,

to abolish systems,
pick up food along the way—
what is useful-.
Find in these books the record,
the stones:
                fossils.
Better listen to the songs.
Why did they sing?
Ease the cables through hawse holes,
hide what was known?
Commentary. Coming after. Blurs.
In *his* story
                he will comment
from a far reach,
try to watch pebbles, or the shape
suddenly shifting out—
smoke/dust.
(Teeth are the hardest.
Often found.)
Fitting a man in there—
breaking the husk—
cracked malt—ferment later—
and the vat gone still.

However he changed things:
Make no judgement,
values in distance
the borders were planted
as he walked.
His cause, his fury.
The dandelion fields,

Aroostook County   carraway and horse radish
along the edge.
There is caution.
These fields are lush with rape.

Carl Ortwin Sauer   He said:
      "We have not yet learned the difference between yield and loot.
We do not like to be economic realists."
                Take that with no question.
                And each step is the restless plunge
                of a conquistador,
                taking for granted the fragile balance.

8

One side of his story—
the one likely to outlast him.
Make it through, then.
Read all the books.
Imagine what can't be done,
and do it.
The sky cracks doom above
a few smoke signals.

Aroostook County   Balm of Gilead,
tree of the north,
begins here.
Somewhere the sweep
of untouched trees,
perhaps the ground birch,
and this one, prostrate,
fragrant as the tundra.
Compression and fusion
the news from there.
Rumors of anger,
that the anger swells
intermittent
            is the voice
which can also sing,
and talk of love.
These things must go on
together,
            or the sense of life
ends.
        In these borders,
north trails perverted,
I see the line that follows now
old boundaries,
water and rock,
            bent,
no matter what the energy
put in.

I follow the wall
this early morning,
sweating as I come out higher.
Field.
        With the bones weathered
as stone,

and these, more recent:
Where a cow dropped.
I go on through mosses,
switch bramble, the woods.
A level floor at times,
holding in its decay,
growing from it.
Will we? from ours?
Grow?
Something other than frost splits,
decayed wood,
weathered bones,
in the mandarin attitude.
"You mean the milk comes
from a cow? I get it
out of a bottle."
Not funny.

Taking the canon law
for text—
or why *do* we wash our hands?
Unclean.
                Thus saith the lord,
but I'd bet on
trichiniae.
(Crow beating his wings
like a broken signpost—
which way is north?)
Get in there and dig!
Well, his story
is for any man.
Make your obeissances.

Edgar Anderson

II

And from that death

                        our sense
of dying.

                 Comes with a rush,
and

      twenty feet of water
where it stood dry
a minute ago.

                  Caught in the flow,
or even in the wind
above it,

          push on and flounder
in a channel,

             adding stems
to current after counter
current.

These years of death,
when death occurs.
The space between deaths,
history of those past.
I cannot take it lightly now.
I grow older, if not old,
and my life, too, is
added to that history.
I have left some middens.
I will add a little more,
and go.

              Has it been that long?
What did I come from?
How many kings have lost their kingdoms?
My smile is still a young man's,
but I know of certain things
less steady—

             and some friends
who seemed to live forever
with me

        gone.
The sense of loss,

            but not
a sense of misery—

George V - Elizabeth II

Charles Olson
Paul Blackburn
Paul Goodman

11

that it all is, really,
sensing.
The real is very small.

(Burrowing a bit to touch ground
as a mole does.
Take his time, and know it.)

Shadowings.
                    The crow on the dead tree
flies away. I do not pursue him.
Shadow wings.

I did not know these men.
I know myself the less—
the lesser part of me.
All I know
                    the sense they leave.
History.
                    Trying to look
at the back of my own head.

To be open and graceful
is not always easy;
to talk of what needs to be talked—
out.
          I fail it every day,
turning away from what most concerns me.
I am afraid of being hurt.
I suppose that's what it means;
but for an example,
The morning's mail brings in
another black-edged letter:
Lee Anderson   "Lee died July 25, 1972."
The friends, and the warmth
of friends, thins and fines,
and to live long is to be alone.
Some of it is selfish.
Perhaps I don't *want* to
talk to these people,
but I know they are there.
Sometimes to see a window lighted
on a dark night,

all that is needed:
So, he's still there.
He hasn't left me.
                    And,
selfish?
It would be good to understand
that selfishness remains
a human virtue—
one of the first of them.,
If I despise myself,
I hate all others.

Moussorgsky,   So, then, I sit here—
    Boris Godounov Pimen, readings,
                    and writing the scrolls of
                    my own   my/his story.

How do I take it all in?
What can I give?

Tempt me a bit more.

I might go on

III

The anger for bereavement:
How dare she leave me?
In all our sense of past,
the most difficult to assess.
The angry widow weeps.
She hates the corpse,
and hates the lost art
to become one.
                    Equals
at that place,
                    she hates
the man she loves.
"How dare he leave me?"

(In a round,
                 everything
reminds me of death.)

That selfishness
becomes / is
a dignity.
Do not stand agaisnt it.
We will go out.
Find another place.
Our grey hair flies
as easily as yours
young flax heads.
Looking for something.
Always looking.
It is good to look at the dead—
the remains of the dead—
to know that a man who died
is not there.

R.T.E.   These are his clothes.
Look at his clothes,
and despite the wound
go away from them
                 more alive.
Tears are not needed,
and if he / she really died,
know that he acted on it—
a full will.

I cannot hold much sympathy
for those agonies
              we bring
upon ourselves.
           The 'mental anguish'
awarded high fees in courts.
There is nothing other in it.
A way to detach—
fly off.
That is important.
Most engaged at a distance.
I *think* I have said things,
but I have lost them,

14

and the loss is of people.
Find where they are.

Voices at full peak—
and we know a way
out.
On the way to a funeral,
pick up a hitchhiker;
the greater honor to the dead.
The past will live
in just such casual acquaintance.
God, as above or below,
in and around it moves,
an arm up stiffly—
a salute to the stars,
or the shadow—
aurora and cloud,
and a sense of the life,
as good damp leaves and wind
rotting—
                a joyous death.
Few walk abroad so late,
but I will be with them,
even as I am alone.

Come where it is comparable
to coming—
go where the ground sheers off,
tread, as if water,
a road in the dark.
(History of these ditches
in mis step may continue:
a broken neck.)
I had realized it solely,
a mention of falling,
coon tumbling asleep from his branch.
The branch falling away from the tree.
(I saw it - no wind.)

The suddenness in bright weather,
shower out of the wind
(from the west)
heading and spreading.

Cut through the woods
exultant—
sleep sound in good air.
But it will not stay,
suddenness breaks out again,
leaves me alone to think
Or tick of the death watch.
His story cuts short.
Well, it was such a day
I went forward
on such a morning,
returned to the shout of elation,
but knew little after:

Isaac Watts   'They fly forgotten as a dream,
before the rising sun.'

"He cometh up, and is cut down like a flower; he fleeth
as it were a shadow, and never continueth in one stay.'

And I went on my way,
out from under the trees.
Tensions set up—
the world, green,
wisps of cloud torn
from the next storm.
(Will it come here?
Has it been?)
At least I will live
'until I die,'
and that death rides with me,
subdued at the moment.
We do not stay long,
nor remember.

I went my own way.

Turned to its resolve,
on day after day—
the attentions for
tight-coiled living.
Yes, it is cold enough
to start fires.
I warm in them,
out of the ashes,

into them again.
The nodes are all fruit,
eaten.
Spit out the seed.
Careless of fortunes,
leave them unburied—
sinking through middens,
eventually the ground closes.

Or as it happens early
on.
Waking—the morning clear,
and sunlight lies
along my face.
I doze.
Then waking clear—in clouds.
The day is covered,
and the sense of strength
is sapped again.
Another one in fear.
Lassitude gnaws the bone.
The visions
        sink.
In this bald way, I know
with whom I travel,
what the history begins,
and why it does.
Yet it is impossible to stay
with it.
This day, too, will clear.
Perhaps in another country,
another day.
I'll go on. The trees
are left behind me now.
Bright enough to see.
What story will I write?
Why will I spend my time
at it?
There is no will,
no ease.
What I write, I write,
in spite of what I do not know.

Speaker and writer in tongues.
I have no knowledge of it.
I am clouded,
embedded in something.
(Day turns pearl.
The grey of a wing—
⎛luminous
⎝unfinished.)

Prisoner along this line.
It is sometimes good,
once against the wall
to go through it—
look back and know,
wondering how—
I *did* come through.
Who made it as it was?
Did no one?
Had I such wisdom?
Only the force—
out of the life,
also the death.
They are the same.
I'm coming in to see
and say it.
Going over hills and walls.
They are the same.
The day may not always move
fast enough.
                    Still,
the day moves.

IV

CENSUS-
con census,
hardly of opinion,
(though it was a guess)
a curiosity—to be known—

it was :
                a spelling—
naming of many
who could not do it for themselves.
Possibly that some would have felt
left out :
                others resisted
for their own reasons,
hid behind snow
and the mud times
-fall or winter- .
'Ford my stream,
or do not come.'
A moat.

"There were, moreover, other difficulties which were of serious moment in 1790, but which long ago ceased to be problems in census taking. The
inhabitants, having no experience with census taking, imagined that some
scheme for increasing taxation was involved, and were inclined to be cautious
lest they should reveal too much of their own affairs, There was also opposition
to enumeration on religious grounds, a count of inhabitants being regarded by
many as a cause for divine displeasure."

Some little distance from opinion—
that which opens up—
and many of the northern counties
ran miles to the sea.
A port for lumber and furs.
A place where a man
coming from 'up country'
might sight the rock
he crawled over,
still wet.

It is said that men in north Franklin County (then Lincoln) went to the
coast with wagons filled with barrels. They dug clams, packed them with wet
sand into the barrels, covered the whole load with kelp, and returned home.
The clams were edible for nearly three months, stored in a cool cellar.

Spirit of the old survives, -
driven into corners,
                at times
persuasive and unbearable—
shadow passes across the sun.

19

Range away—
an exorcism
rising from the fog.
A long and bitter night for sailors
still at sea.
Tempted by the sounds of names
a man might conjure up
a graveyard. It would
stick with him—.
North New England!   where it
stays the longest,
scent of a dead hand
in the dying leaves.
(Sundays. One senses them.
Ghosts of Puritans still stalk
these woods,
look in with disapproval—
grim.
They cannot face us,
but they hate our guts.
Our day must rise
                    slowly
from the ashes of the night.)

ARIA

Temporal illusion:
That what is termed forever,
projected from a thumbprint,
is only the thumbprint.
That moment the cosm.
A permanence of story
held by inconstant files
of remembrance;
and in the most serious thinking,
I know its worth.
One peak of emoion
poured out/
cannot sustain itself out
nor can I—
have reached the end of it—
possibly should have kept
my / mouth / shut.

L.B.   8/26/72

20

But from its fragility,
the faint odor of perfumes—
the lingering of delight
in tenderness—
what two friends,
no lovers,
may say to each other
in the dark.
The permanence remains there
and no regret,
nor attempt to make more of it
than it is.
That gentleness of touch—
fingers against hair

                  and

goodnight.

Moving back from it,
what were the reasons?
What spells did they set,
as they spelled?

                out?

'Gra'   enough.
(A cipher that the lord did not
discover their names listed?)

    And in Bristol Town there were a number who did not capitalize their
names as: moody, umbehind, hall, hussey and wolts—turney, becker, and
hatch. A brotherhood, or a spelling out?

High in the back country
where I sit

           now,

the water flows to the sea—
seeps under

           and over

the rocks   gathering
force and volume,

              linking

and binding me

              to the shores

I came from,

           the far promises

laid out—
        the county
and plantation.
          Men knew it
then
        they held in their frosts
the sense of the tides—
kelp smell and salt
against moon
        against sun.
The pull of the rise
          and the ebb.
A simple thing—
seeing it so.
A simple place,
and yet uncommon now.
The north counties
no longer run
        to the sea.
Cut off, their affairs close in
and center alone—
at their peril.

I always had
an eye for land,
as another might
have said
     for *her*:
The body of a woman,
as the land stretches out
into the night
away from me
-to be pursued-
at all costs to be made
my own.
Even then,
        I knew
that it could not be—
and that I would never own
what I had an eye for.
It comes to me
now,

and I *have* an eye for it—
running beyond my grasp.

It was from the sea
I took my hunger,
crushed more
than I could keep.
I went on
            daily
over the barrens,
through these lost counties.
I knew them.
They surely knew me.
The voices of the dead
answered in parts.

Went inside,
broke sticks
            and
started a fire.

V

Then.
Had you heard it?
The sound of the past
dragging its chains
over the faces of men living?
No way to escape.
No certain way out.
We all hear the past—
rumbling in cellars
at midnight—
free stone falling
in frost season—
out of it.
Dust whispering along
our veins,
imitating pulse and blood,

but so dry!
We turn dry
almost before   we knew
that we grew up.
It is the sound of *our* death,
as well as past death.
It becomes confused
with a history,
which, at its best,
it is not.
We listen to it
at our peril.
It begins with,
'Do you remember?'
His story does,
too,
but the news is other.
It is altered.
It is different,
and we rarely in range
to find or view it.

"And the rains came,
and the winds blew,
and they beat upon that house.
Great was the fall thereof."
(And it made no difference
what it was founded upon.)
The joy must be
in the thing itself—
not in its use.
We are fed into the hopper
of history.
We know it for no other reason,
and we die.
Few ways to get around that.
We urge ourselves
forward,
          and go back.
Crumble into proper dust.
Voiceless.
(And the rains still beat
upon that house.)

I have stood on
the edge of catastrophe
more times than I needed,
knowing that it was risk,
and that I would lose.
It is the same with
a marriage.
One never knows,
and should not.
                    Oh,
that comfortable place
where some are willing
to lose themselves:
"A business relationship",
"Partnership"
                    whatever glib despair
glosses it over
and seals its failure,
as it seals the failed
from living.
I cannot hold to that.
I stand on the brink
                    daily
knowing
that I may fall down.

No one listens.
The voices are indistinct,
but they are real—
ominous rumbles at all points
of reference—
east or north—
the ones I listen for . .
The mill in the next town
Forster Mfg. Co.,   sounds through the wind
Strong, Maine   on the ridges.
Not my news,
but some men listen
and reorder their lives
by it.

The differing spellings:
One name—

25

a single family:

Maine Census: "Jealoson, Jealouson,
1790   Jellitson."

(Whose son had care of what?
What jealous care?)
Still ready for me—
dead voices
coming into live:

There are those who feel
deeply,
         as my father,
the loss of those
who cannot be
made up to them.
(More active, the guilt)
He says of dreams:

T.V.E.   'My father came to me,
looking for securities,
those that I had
               administered,
and I froze in bed.'
Later, of my mother:

R.T.E.   'She was standing
in the corner of the room,
looking through her jewel boxes.
Everything was gone.
I had given it—
and even though I had given
to those she would have wanted,
I felt that sense of guilt.'
'I was in some sense
both murderer and thief.'
These things are more than dreams.

It is hard to go on.

We go on.

The feet of the darkness.
Why one says that,
headfirst,

It is harder in this way
to reach over—
but one reckons.
It is evident,
clearly
and easily.

(The wind—
past my window—
(wind's eye—
brings in the smoke.
I sense the aging
of the year—
each fall of ash.

Hardly made for it—
but on the verge
of something other.
Walking on—
making the most of
what went before.
(But the past can numb.
Catch your feet
in a vise.)
His story—
　　　　　something else—
again
　　　　and again,
hurries and hammers in.
What will they tell us?
nothing much more worth hearing.
All of a piece.
But today I saw something:
above the late mandrake,
sium and baneberry
where the two brooks merge—
at a certain water,
the flow opposes:
flat calm for,
　　　　　say,
a table's length.
Something in all those years
I've passed by

Conant Bridge,
10/10/72

27

not noticing.
The opposition is there,
as it is in our lives—
the healthy thrust
that keeps us living.
(What will they tell me?)

And of those late poisons,
mandrake and sium,
white baneberry,
hardly much news,
except that they survive,
and in better ways than we do.
I coiuld take them
hardly much news,
except that they survive,
and in better ways than we do.
I could take them
lying in cold shadows
with the wind,
and laugh.
(In open fields
closed in with alder,
the sun burns hot,
but there is an iron bite
-new winter-
on the way.
Well, I am uncertain.
The brooks flow.
The winds blow,
and men curse themselves
while knowing it.

VI

CASSIOPEA.
(In her chair
above this roof—
peak - at gable end -

I've seen her twice
in four nights.
Cassiopea, the queen.)

What a way to begin it!
The winter nights
in the old place,
and on the mountain.
I fly free.
Again and again,
tongues of metal
against the cold.
Once, my accidental mountain.
Now, all of a purpose.
To listen to the streams below.
To know that this is where I belong.

One could hardly say
or not say
that a spatter of acorns
counted little.
Or that the wind whistled
around the candle
one night when I worked late.
Simply, I cam back
to where I belong.
(A great deal could be destroyed.
But I see little of that.
What I say, I see.

(Later on—
as another night makes—
—across the wind—
the final, legal, shot of the day.
Reverberates—
almost as starshine
makes out of the hills.)

Complicates it:
Earlier, the Ethiopian Queen—
her knees planted—
lap spread amply
in a north sky.

(A capful of wind
is a hatful of stars,
a pailful reflected
on the verge of the pond.
The way out—
the stance outward.
Breath! breath for the night.
It breathes, and the dark
is in/to us.
We made out time.
His story told itself.

The strong sidereal pull
which lasts into
the cold days following—
excitement of the wind
above the ridges,
dying into silence in the dark
until the stream below
picks it up—
s p a c e d the stars
                              across
a lighter sky,
now,
and below
the first full snow.
It fell,
and left us unaware.

Reiterates:
The final, legal shot of the day.

Lights like costain flares.
The sea of these cold hills—
the waves that break.
Evoke them.
The breathless passage.
It is there,
climbed over.

And I speak of
rooms swept bare,
lying in moonlight—

of the sun
that comes up from snow hills,
breaking—
          always the breaking
to make a day.
My fortune contemplates,
               and
you must receive it.
Are we doing
         any?
thing?
So bright - above us -
C A SS I O P E A .

VII

If I had had the price,
if there *were* a price,
or had it been given
without price.
          Not easy
to come clear on this.
The sensible 'law':
everything has its price,
comes back to me.
But I have not believed it.
At odd times tried,
          and failed.
No, it doesn't stick,
except inthe craw
with a fishbone.
A price? Well, take my head,
or cock, and fix a value.
None, except to me.
Take the drift of talk—
the ordinary, simple, speech,
reasonable men relaxing,
confident of price,

but lost to fit it.
What is it worth?
                    Yes,
but not a rate of exchange.
Some other things exchanged
for love.
Impregnate the universe,
and then,
be on your way.
Difficult - beset -
beyond besetting.
Taken in time, but always
the querulous:
How much?
It is the history of times,
a block of stone or iron
for a cow.
(The weight's the same—
equals?)
How did you hit this tack?
and if you did,
how long before another?
I completed little.
Preferred not to sell.
I can't talk much
to other men.
They refuse to believe.
By their lights,
a possibility.
Men will talk this through.
Others will ask
for a bill of sale.
Men calculating.
Let them.
The rest of us,
whoever we are,
live on their margin—
away from them.
(What palms, not greased)
grow sweaty from a hold
on rope
or steering wheels?

What ship, following the night,
slips out?)

Made this deal with the wind,
see,
a whole truckload of orders
blowing in from the west
and the north.
Cold morning—rings steel
from ice along my boots,
chop it from the frozen pail—
a little water left
in the middle of it.
Precious liquor—
can't be had for price.
I went out in the morning,
but I came back shortly,
and lay down to rest.
The buzz of their busyness—
quarrels/

       /anvils/

muffled.
I didn't hide from them,
but left them all behind.
I had a good place,
and held on to it.
'But if the price is right,
you sell anything.'
The mark of astute dealing.
I went back again
to the wind,
and,
his story told of that.
Kingdoms fell,
but they had no business to be
in the first place.
Counting houses pitched over,
and even the corner grocery
a lie.
I had it from one
that he sold and bartered
for social change.

I listened, but I remained
unconvinced.
And he was, too,
sadly holding the bag.
Change, whatever it is,
comes inside
one man at a time.
Taken over again,

Blackenstryk Dream   I move away,
possessed with myself.
Many times that energy
to perform its will.
Came out—clear morning.
Stood looking down the wind
for sounds—
                        nothing.
A few clouds to the south—
a high, thin cirrus,
and perhaps a storm
tomorrow.

(Through it—
the stumps and roots—

to Montreal 12/3/72   old mountains tumbling
in the frost.
Worn to the gums,
they die—away—
trip north in winter
without price
or such attachment.)

Conversation   The rasping voices
        overheard   breaking in again:
Groveton,   "Well, if a man cuts my trees
    New Hampshire   I can take him into district court—
    12/3/72   charge triple damages.
Don't pay to cut a tree
on someone else's land
these days."
"Yeah, but it don't grow
the trees back.
Takes twenty years."
"So what, I'd get

34

triple damages!
Fifty dollar tree,
that's a hundred fifty bucks."

(And he wrote me:
"If the earth had all been
flat plains
would men have built
the mountains?")

H.S.

Always the voyage—
more to less.
The end completes
as it cannot—
fades out:
        (Echo)
"Will it pay?"

              aye

VIII

Samuel de Champlain:
Des Sauvages

To speak of 'Les Sauvages.'
Perhaps he did not need
a voyage to New France,
but I am grateful that he went,
and touched exactly
                on the place—
the people in it—
            rivers
that flowed out of
          the land,
beyond the reach of men
in boats.
        Only the Algonkins
in canoes
        had known them.
Lakes on lakes—
          islands
in those rivers—

                    aits
of pleasant prospect,
woods and vines and
fertile meadows.
Regrettable the hope
that these would tame
and yield.
                    He could not
think of that,
                    talking with Le Sieur du Pont,
West of Tadoussac,
and back again
                    in early summer—
cold and niggardly,
                    and then alive
again.
          Wondering, but scanting
in the records.

The clouds do break
in south and west—
the winter sun
a frozen guest.

To the relief of all the crew,
arrived back safely
in the fall at Havre de Grace.

And now,
                    Les Sauvages have fled,
lost,
somewhere north,
along that 'salt arm
of the Atlantic'
splitting a continent in half.
Cree
Ojibwe
Algonkin—
the native Ihalmiut.
The remnants of nations
foraging to keep alive,
with no clear reason
for it.

Hudson Bay

Something of that flows down
the arctic wind
this winter—
voices—ghosts—
apples frozen on a few gnarled trees.
Shattering on snow crust—
the skulls—
the hopes within them
scattered on these bitter nights.
Damp wood that keeps men chilled
despite the flame.
Shaking a head,
listening to harsh sounds,
the voices whistling cheer
against the wind.

Why did we come this far?
What will the north bring?
Top heavy balance
that rubbed out good places,
left their slag behind
to bleach and sink.
(Little rots here.
Bones of the past break up,
and mark the tent rings
in an empty land.)

Cut and rape.
Kill and mine—
and then—get out.
That history is open,
and that past is past.
In the name of kings
our heritage.
Carved bones and teeth
in dusty cases.
A few men die
still.
Each candle
of their lives—flares—
and then goes out.
The islands are not pleasant.
The vines died long ago.

New winds come down
across the northern shield—
and they are tinged with blood
that never knew the wind.

Lament - lament,
but whose lament?
for what?
The remnants of great herds
each spring.
The fear of wolves—
a sentimental talking.
Warned—forewarned—
deaf,
      and even the dead
lie upwards and unburied.
No casting of accounts—
it ends in questions.
The pale men build,
and then abandon what was built.
The snows pile bolts of shroud,
rot down,
and pile again.

(A short history of the weather
breaks in.
The hatred in that snow!
It fell across us
without pity,
without reason,
and we attempted to make
reasons for it.
It was a time—
a point in nowhere—
a long way from nothing—
a long way through
             nothing.
And perhaps nothing
beyond that.
We attempted to break
the land.
We opened it up,
emptied it of its

heart and liver.
We were so certain
that we had reasons.
We fought the weather,
and our blunt tools
and broken axe handles
remain.
((Les Sauvages were wiser.
Except for colonies
along the rivers,
near the coasts,
they never lived here—
passed through on hunting expeditions
in the spring and summer.))
We built our farms
here—
          tilled whatever
flat land was available,
built our houses on ridges
to escape floods,
but didn't escape them.
We knew so *well*
what we were doing.
Some of us learned
all of us died here
eventually.
Our sons took off,
and our barns and houses
broke under weight of snow
a few years later.
It snowed from nowhere
to nowhere—
a point in time
that vanished
before it began.
We would all do well
to set sail for
Havre de Grace.

Admiring these people
—Les Sauvages—
and dismissing them
as beneath contempt

in a breath—
as 'crude and
stupid'
            because of beliefs
which were centered
in the land
                in what they knew
in the land,
not in the wisdom
of Rome and Christendom.
It has led us
a long way.
We have found nothing
but defeat.
Now, too late,
and our cellar holes
rank with the tent circles.
We destroyed ourselves,
and we destroyed them.
We have gone into darkness,
and we will not come back.

The voyagers didn't know.
Would they have cared?

Snow falls this year
the snow
            snow
only the snow

IX

So, to have been beaten, out,
the year begins at year's end,
darkened by the death, the wounds,
the sense of somewhere—
nothing new, and nothing old.
And I walk out on Pittston Hill,
alone, and in a winter rain.

Pittston, Maine.
January, 1973

40

In fog,
lights touching inthe branches.
Church hulk hunkering
below dead elms.
I walk this way, and back
again from back.
It is hard to walk the first time,
and walk it in the rain.
It is hard, I say,
and in this softness, harder—
dampness and the partial thaw—
a sea storm in again,
and almost close enough to taste the salt.
How little taken!
For its bitterness, a tonic,
eating of old roots for pain.
The new bud slices off; is
lost in its own blood.
An exile hurrying along
this way—
                    goes on
to such another.
(One more church spire—
truncated in the wind—
a ladder leaning and askew
inside the belfry.)

Now, on another morning—
pale winter sun,
its water squeezing
through dead shards of cloud—
a strength of iron—
fragile to a blow—
substantial as it strikes
an attitude.
Why am I here?
What do I make of it?
Why?
The winter lag of time
from no
            time
to no
        other.

Why am I here?
A pain in questions:
To wait it out—
a notch each day,
as each one passes.
Winter sagging
at my seams.
It pulls. Pervades.
It dies,
          but doesn't.
All around us, and
another storm is due
tomorrow.
On the inside, weather,
stuck like burs.
Day by day it changes,
slowly.
          Light comes longer
in the afternoons.
Orion stepping to the west.
A simple tilt,
a flow of ocean currents.
It was a land of corn and wine,
before it turned to ice.
Implicit on the rocks—
that something lived
more gently here.

Well, what about all this?
I sit inside
against a creeping cold.
(as well that I have come
up here
          in silence)
The sun lights up
a cruel pattern
                    deftly notched—
of cold and frost.
the outline of a shed that burned—
now shivering in the cold.
I look above it—
one strange cloud in wind—
its center gone—

an eye—
            the vortex,
one small storm that vanishes
before it makes.

What I have tried,
each time I come to this:
A figured speech—exact—
that clarity which says
itself—
and is the only reason
for our speaking.
It is *hard* to put this down—
to know that in the putting
it exists at all.
Our tools are ciphers
that surround—
the emptiness of that still pool
within the cloud.
To be aware of this—
to go beyond it,
but to, so, contain it,
makes a history
within itself.
I know no other way.
The storm is spoken
in its breathless center,
and the winds stream out
in dissipated fury.

Those nights in winter—
days in summer—
measure of their season.
By them, the history completed.
All on the edge of being—
broken and piled—
so many ledges of dark ice
along a ploughed road.
But,
        pried loose,
or open,
            one survives.
The end of it is

G.O.
Of Being Numerous

nothing easily impelled—
applied.
How a man takes
into himself the hurt,
and uses it.
Thus he might make
of misfortune certain contacts—
the touch and go
-generative power.
Then I move beyond it,
find myself among the living—
Incredibly alive.
Foundered on woe—
the least of it—
to spring up.
Progression of these days.
Complaint of limbo,
but it isn't here:
in us, that loss.
The days will see us safely through,
or in their dangers,
destroy us.
A firm grasp, always.

John Muir at Yosemite,   Help me up—
       1869   to look over the falls
from a three inch heel seat,
into the heart of them.
Only, there is no help—
the body involved.
One loses identity,
looks and leaves the rest
to take care of itself.
An easy ascent
over—
            one way to look
in perspective.
"And the ground falls away
at your feet—
                    sheer drop,
and a shatter."
What is it that leads us
to the top edge—

44

always—
when the bottom is obvious,
and easy?
To retrieve
the center, stand
above it,
            centered.
Rooted in places
that are not
            easy
to root in—
            places
that are not.
            Intuit
those that are.
Crushed in the rubble,
bits of past strata.
To go there,
begin where you are.
I had leave of this
before I knew it.

As an imperative:
I am here.
            You are
here or there.
Neither of us
stands outside.
Yet I deduce
that you and I
are here / there.
Anywhere the cold wind
blows in again,
cares nothing for us,
is clear in that.
We do not will life
into
        what lives
for itself.
So, I will saddle myself
with the earth—
a beam as lever
breaks in my hand.

I am the lever,
all moves because of me,
because of all, I move.
Despite,
        and in despite.
The teeth of the matter
are open jaws—
walk gingerly,
find toe hold,
thumb latch.
Move up across
the face of the rocks,
adhesive.
Well, many days to come,
and this grave sunlight
peers over my shoulder.
Broken clouds, aloft,
a good day in passage.
Better that I go outside
than sit inside in heat,
and freeze the blood.

X

Into and
        out of
these woods.
As I grow older, I become
restless,
        more than I was.
it is hard to take
one place for pivot—
knowing that all are centered,
and that I must move
from one center to
another—
        merely that.
Sun flares against

46

the back of my hand,
warmed by the glass
it comes through.
(Into and
        out of
these woods again.)
Stood watching the set
last night on Pittston Hill—
across the dead river
mottled in ice and dark snow.
A hard time of year,
but the life is stirring
behind closed doors
and bare branches.
Into and
        out of
these woods.)

Down over the hill,
and under the trees,
equals
down over the trees
and under the hill—
inside the trees as locus—
pro tem the center—
being—
more than being.
I walked there in the last light,
wondering at chill.
And the shout of it,
rising from me,
unheard
        except
that my ears rang
at the place where my voice
cracked.
I saw myself over.
I saw myself through.
And yet I was alone with this.
I talked to some
I didn't know.
They knew me,
but couldn't hear the words.

It was my way in,
as well,
pushing the snow
from my feet.
Listening a bit.
A hard day in winter,
but relaxed—
and I fell asleep.
Into and out of these woods
again,
          the sound of it
depends upon aging—
something not yet seen—
the center, shifting surface,
always the center.

John Muir   'Shapeless harvests of revealed glory,
                             but with a shape
                             buttoned down
                             to the angle of the earth.
                             Impossible to move away—
                             shaped.

Pittsston Woods   And in the forest,
hemlock stump   that old pollard buttressed
                             against the winter ground,
                             brown iron to white iron,
                             curious in design,
                             curved over—
                             bent—split—
                             and living, fresh as the twitch
                             of a new frond.
                             Centered.
                             Took leave of that one—
                             went out with it—
                             passing of a storm.

                             Days when I felt inside it,
                             days, alone, outside.
                             Days of guilt, when I
                             could not feel that
                             I had added much—
                             all days of history—
                             one thing after another.

All that was needed.
We do not make it of
large things.
Smaller than ways into,
we come outside.
It is assessed by weight of days,
the sap of trees in aggregate,
weight of the sea.
Detritus of lives
pushed from us,
within sight.
We try to turn away
from it.
We cannot.
The days are richer and brighter—
our leavings stain them.
Do not attempt to leave me behind.
I stain too.
Shatters / like / glass /
the day's brightness
opens and shines,
but the cold inside it
is dark cold.
It does not die.
We thing it does,
holding that dark core
in silence.
Well, I think, I've thought,
broken through,
something that for me
is good—or goodness,
taking what is live,
as dead at such a place,
in catches.
Take this cold,
some place it stays alive,
at some such other place
tightens / chills / chips.
A further point—
the glass clears,
leaves out colors
as that stain—refines—

distills—
        only
the wind blowing over
the high land—
hollows and fortunes'—
Howls - dead.

Cleared of the element,
as water from cast bergs,
floating away from the tide waves,
outward and down-fjord,
tensed in south rain,
clear again.
Cryptic and stiff,
the design left to follow.
Outside, the deep freeze
rising.
Came around to the other side,
storm bent to
its own end—
lightening of clouds,
and the rain.

To have the bolt of cloth,
begin with thread,
stitched over as many times
as it may be.
The thread remains.
Essence distilled,
it comes from the stain
of doing.
Do not cover it.
(I sensed my way
out of axioms.)
Came up early enough.
The day was dull
as any other,
felt my passage
inandoutofthewoods,
a fusion dealing
with it.
That old pollard, say,
hung over,

Pittston hemlock

at the edge of the woods,
left only because
it seemed useless.
The cutters walked by.
Several times
they felled the forests
around it,
were hardly aware
that it stayed on
and seeded other trees,
now boards and beams
for many years.
Brood sense of the woods,
avoiding history
in new lives.
Whatever it was
I took out of the woods
beyond the scent-resin
and crumpled bark,
I left some there.
Footprints in fresh snow.
No one may know them
after the first thaw,
but the footprints go down
into the duff,
twist new life
in ways it cannot know.
The individual quirk
laid on—
ancestral by another species.
They grow taller
than their fathers—
rich on decay—
but dying earlier,
fall, in the first winds.
We make it slowly
over old bodies—
verdigris.
Can't come in on this
any other way.
Hands stained in mud
are stained on life—

do not wipe them.
(His saws.)
Stand out of the way.
We came up,
and as we are cut down,
we come up again—
another form.
Still, that old pollard
in the wood
bothers me:
Out of what time she came,
what time she nurtures?
None that I know—
my measure to myself,
and here, near to the life
below the skin.
Dark days I go there,
looking,
only the swelled moss
holding on.
They tempt me into places
I have never known before,
vaguely realized
in faces at the back of
my head,
a place I cannot journey
or find the news.
It lies contiguous,
on another plane.
Ancestral stain,
I might talk about it,
but in terms that do not fit
exactly.—
brother only to the shards
which do not live there,
any more than I do.
North clouds floating—
thin, and breaking up.
A wet walk, if it is
once more
into and
          out of
these woods.

XI

I did not climb to the height
of such powers—
nor look down from them.
They happened—
                    suddenly,
and were gone,
                    coming back,
an increasing strength
in them.
They will subside.
Perhaps a hint, and meaning,
when I return to places
written out,
and talk about them:
'Remember the Joanna poem?
It was near here.
Perhaps the height implied—
sustaining wing power—
or a lookout.
(Only for a moment,
that bloodshot sun—
but in the morning,
on the rise.
I look for darkness
early,
        and a storm.)
Easy to tell when power
is gone,
or when it sits with others.
Had to hold on.
It comes and it goes,
but it goes *where* it goes.
I climbed, but not there.

If I have learned any one thing,
the interruptions are not all
from Porlock,
nor are these 'persons'
always the devil.
I can include them—

Between Eagle and
Cupola, Pa.

2 miles to Cupola

D.L.

get them in / to,
with all their baggage,
usually find what they
interrupted
in the process.
It's all a hard way in,
but probably harder
in loneliness—
the craft to be alone
in the midst of,
wherever the distractions
build most.
The dams are choked
with weeds,
but more than that:
a presumption of what
weeds are.
I'll draw you on.

A night. A mask
of fevers—
whatever it is
that holds a man to bed,
to dreaming—
Construction of what he has—
living / lived.
Whatever he'll build
outside of that—
if he survives.
I'll draw you on.
But he must imprison
and hold onto
the interruptions.
In this way
I'll draw you on.
Grateful for that wisdom,
for one who doesn't believe it.
A whole history—
well—
what would history be like,
and art,
if it were't for Porlock—

and all the men
that come from there?
It's always been
an excuse for inattention,
convenient,
rarely examined.
Perhaps our only duty now
is to incorporate it—
the pearl
from that grit of sand.
Heed me,
but not for wisdom,
only for this blunder
which turned out.
A map of Porlock,
larger than any world
we knew before.
Strange contours—
the motion
over the centers,
guided by rhythms
of embarassment and distaste.
Well, it'll be good enough
to hold onto.

The dream cut off,
ends at exactly the point
where it should end.
Remember that, too.
None of the anger
or exasperation will bring it
back alive:
Rough ends and leave them
rough.
Few other dreams
so memorable.
All we have to do is climb,
and keep on climbing,
to reach anywhere
we might want to go
from anywhere we might want to leave—
touch in—
touch out—

Paraphrase of Mao's
second Chengkang
Mountain poem

or cut the mountains down
to bite size—
not for men - but for
themselves, and concepts
of themselves.
Writes its way out so fully,
easily puts itself
at my hand.
(And the mountain rises
out of a continent named Porlock.)
No one's ever called all this
into question,
just taken it for granted—
and swatted at mosquitoes
on a hot night.

Somebody looking over my shoulder,
and sharing the news—
well, why shouldn't he?
Why shouldn't I share?
despite the place where
I am and was.
Do I think it's my news?
Can I control it
that much?
I think I can at times??
But the man still looks.
He is my guest.
(All we had to do
was change a few letters
from ghost.)
Certainly I've held on
long enough to be able
to say these things
straight.
Used to cost me more
to lie about it,
and pretend to enjoy
what I despised.
O.K. I've said it this way
now, and to my cost.
what will I, or you,

Or anyone do
about it?
Diminishing the road
or role—
the embarassment of return—
"But don't you love
the place of your birth?
Your origins? All men do."
(All men don't.
I will choose whatever place
I want, to claim for birth.
Ancestry I mistrust.
I may be interested
for a moment in it—
but what about that flood-flecked sun
that came up yesterday?
Did I ever see that before?
Gentlemen, here is the map
of that new city-state:
Porlock.

XII

SACROSANCTUS * * *
yet believing—
where, outside, I get the
sense—the
movement over,
oracle and ritual.
I make it in.
I deem it holy.
Write
as you find it-
-in your heart-
to write."
Anything more difficult.
more simple
Hard to find.

But to find the heart—
a man, a race,
goes far—
out on the limb,   ,
to the back of the limb,
to a place
where no place
adds itself to place
where:

Edward Kelly,
the Alchemist

'I venture to hope, however,
that my life and character
will so become known
to posterity
that I may be counted
among those who have suffered
much for the sake of truth."
A simple fee statement
in such obscurity.
(Whatever does the man want?)
parenthetical statement—
the arms—
arms of the man
in orison.
A statement of Tao—
all in parenthesis.)))))))
To force your attention.
Time ripe and rife
for that—
ornate escutcheon—
only to make sense
of it.
The, whenever.
A time for it
when a man
is not simply
a doer or maker,
and the poet
sits down with the lamb.
I look for it. All of us—
good men, and the like,
fining in shades
to darkness—

the
white (light)
becomes here,
passing / passim—
do
out of doing—
senses in the stone
only to be deciphered.
Venture this—
remembering interpretation,
the free use
of history—
from its associations.

Born free enough
to say these things
clearly.
Brave challenge.
(That's the darkness
out there.)
and you'd best heed it,
more than better.
Making a portion of the day
up.
Said sometimes
that a man changes once—
if he changes—
a chance and
rarely a possibility.
It would come, perhaps,
in middle age—
his—
and no one else's.
His time being his
own sense of time,
which, if he followed it,
would be
        what it finally is—
a tide calendar,
adjusted—
certain hours and minutes,
to lattitude—

bays, coves, and bores,
north fjords—
wherever *he* is,
a pronouncement.
His SACRO

SANCTUS.

And outside,
             to take the sense:
Swing the old noose
over a neck,
and watch it break.
It does.
             more often than a heart;
the bone more fragile
than the muscle.
Intended (this)
or any other way.
A tide calendar is a tight one.

Schedules made over,
tucked into the degree
of movement—
the sacred moment,
as one man moves
across the floor.
A death stroke
which heals—
raises up
what *seems* to be dead.
The days have it with us,
not, as we think,
in our divisions.
Time is that tribal chieftain
with many names.
One, it says to no one
The name itself
inherent
in the stream.
The day acknowledges,
and then goes down.
Putting these papers
in an order

Professor Cheng
Man Ch'ing

somewhat *inside*,
makes privacy
the darkness,
but it says nothing
of the papers—
what they will for
themselves.
Daily I put myself
to one task
or another—
and I do not know
the sense of what I do.
The circle,
and the square and
the core
remain intact—
a sanctity,
a sanctity from what
I might bring to definition.

Trying the wave—
but each time it is easier
simply to look on—
to see how *she* sleeps.
Not to wake her—
for more reasons than a mere
disturbance.
She sleeps /
        I wake.
same time.
The breathless plunge
into it
is more than quiet—
what moves inside
remains an outer calm.
Monet: Those lillies—
Waterlillies   that water—
this distance.
I look up carefully
from the papers
for the spell.
I may not have read it
in its context;

but the day is fresh.
It opens
                into
orison.

XIII

How difficult it is!
How strange to break in
on the self   on those sections
of self that lie buried
but so vulnerable
that a footstep above them,
on loose-packed detritus,
hurts to the quick,
and makes life of
pain—that it lives—
at all lives.
So I have heard of one more—
perhaps the first woman

L.E.S.
I knew as a woman—
gone away, and now dead.
We speak briefly
of the dead,
as if we no longer wanted
to think of them,
but their presence is
none the less—
living in some other place.
We stay with them.
Ancestors in that tree,
or the corners of the room—
ploughed over and over
to raise grain.
It is no good thing to move
away from them.

Vietnamese Ritual
If we move, we strap
old bones upon our backs,

and take them as more valuable
than what we lead.
Carry Anchises—
take Ascanius by the hand.
The steepness leads
into the bowels of the earth—
below the place
we came from—
the hill town above
a bright cenotaph
dead, in the flaring sunlight,
despite time of day.
It won't do to face it,
crane the neck to look back.
Worse fate than a pillar of salt
waits for those
who try to.

Well, in each trial there is
something left—
something to take forward:
'borrowed and blue.'
The old rituals read in strange places.
Wind at the top of the draw,
silence of night broken
only by the loose drop
of a stone or gravel
over.

Comes to the eye
out of focus—
the remnant—
frame of the picture
I look through—
unset—but solid—
there.
     As vacant
looking back from itself:
a frame of light.
An instant, unimportant,
thence—
       and not to be forgotten.

Perhaps as a form of dedication,
a man dares go no further
than his woman,
that it should all be given
there—even if—
(allegedly it is, in most cases)
it is not understood
or much wanted—
not wanted, say,
in the same sense
that wood and water is,
or in an age of exchange:
Money.
That it becomes money of a sort—
specie—
often presented with a hangdog look
of unworthiness—
a hope that the giver
will not be beaten
for time spent
in such unprofitable work.
Then:
We will fuse this with the woman:
Earth,
            μήτηρ γή
and I give the Greek,
since it symbolizes other
than Mother Earth.
We flow there on a lazy river
back—
when we sensed kobolds and nixies
as the real,
                    small gods of the real—
Rudolf Hauschka: and not those brother metals
The Brothers of Iron   in all their heaviness—
cobalt and nickel.
Whatever harshness squeezed out—
we make of it,
it is merely the difference
overlaid
between our world and that dim one,
passed through.

We may not go there again
except through the refining light
of our own material age.
Our history—reduction to that one—
to grasp both as present—
to live with the past.
To align both
in such a solid air.

XIV

When I had the process
fully in hand
I was no longer living—
I had gone
into another place—
a place not believed in.
There was no need
for belief.
Freedom, Maine   I found, on this plane,
the town of other dimensions.
It does exist,
and people walk there.
The town clerk winds his watch,
remembering the births
and marriages of all that live there.
Careful man.
At the moment,
whatever mastery it held,
to realize that I had had the sense
of substance—
and the care of it—
no more than that.
That all was noble metal—
of ceremony.
I did not own it.
Only such things
as were lost forever
became a part of me.
They were few,
are not remembered,

and these others pass on
to be handled and worn away
by those I will never see
or know—.

Breaks in suddenly,
tearing the roots of thinking
away by their flesh:
"Well, what of this history:
'I did,'
       'He did,'
its meanings, and various portions
of truth or untruth?
What about these?
is it a body produced,
or one lent and passed on?
Can one weight it?
Does it reduce in heat
to a powder—
red or white?
St. Dunstan's Fire?
What sort of mixing?
Who is in spell, or free."
And I drop it all as stealing.
It is not the living bone.
In one such book:
"But do not say too much, Kelly;
for ahead smoke ascends
in the distance
from the roofs of houses,
and the shadows of the hills
begin to lengthen."
More dangers than we know
in telling the whole story—
blueberry field, clam flat,
or a mystery of gold.
Spending the morning at it,
I bring judgement to bear
on one small place,
whatever the elixir.
The tools that made it
are broken,
and the door swings in the wind

Edward Kelly:
The Humid Path

from the workhouse.
(I spent the evening,
the day will be easier.
Difficult to get at
the crabbed lines,

Constantine Hering's
copy of the
Ortis Sanitatis
1520

the daubed figures—
'spelta' 'nux vomica'
'tenacetum.'
Works of the monks, evidently,
Their lost proportions.
Let out the stale air.
Better. Go outside.

At that moment, a break
in tension—
something that let out,
loosened the strings.
I saw that *thing* come
down the road, vomitting exhaust,
out of place—
its or ours,
              and Jake said,
"A big yellow!"
meaning anything with shovels
or rollers that's supposed
to do the present work of the world.
I could argue that point—
and since it was dark,
I can't say that it *was* yellow.
Some of them are green,
even red,
but it came, and with the noise
always brings me.
There was also release.
How often can a man say that?
I was worrying the bone
of old histories—
suddenly I was let loose again.
I didn't have to do it,
or think it, any more.
Something gave me the way.
I could go down the street

with my hands on my hips—
set 'slonchways',
warnin' 'em all
to get the hell out of my way.
(But prob'ly I didn't need to—
just felt that I had my hand
on things there.)
That's a hard way to start it,
but it always happens
when we least expect it to.
(After a little while,
they loaded the 'big yellow',
and took it away.)

I motioned to myself to
stop talking until I knew
something better to talk about,
but the habit was so
deeply a part of my nature,
the reflex stopped.
In tension
became intention.
I looked out at the graveyard
and thought of snow.
The snow *was* the graveyard,
old bones rotting down
from the top—
                too easily.
Well, the whole year
turns on that,
            and as
a child says,
"Look, it's a big yellow!"

XV

It is not the interruption
we complain of,
                    but the inability
to cope with more than one
sound at a time,
or more than one direction—
seeing out—
                    the sense outraged
-maybe not the senses-
what we have done with them,
ordering them to align
like a trawl line set at sea,
so that the hooks don't snarl—
from the killick anchor
to the dolicky rock—
strung and paid out.
Maybe our ancestors did it
better? with no preconception
of how much a man could profitably
take in at a time—
or what directions he should take
to begin with.
(I don't know that any of this
is so, but it's worth
speculation—
                    like the morning
itself—dark and forbidding—
fog hanging over the sea.
I know that several miles

Pemaquid Point
3/16/73

to the east, there is an island—
Allen's Island, which I have seen
on clear days. Maybe it's a relief
that I don't see it now,
left alone with the fog's edge,
and the sea—the waves softened
in damp air and grey light.
Only this small segment of sea,
close and intimate, so that I
don't need to think of it
in terms of thousands of miles,

islands in between, and other shores
with galaxies of weather,
storms, and clear places, perhaps—
simply to overlook
my knowing or telling of it.
I'm not sure how
the totality would be,
if all of it should strike me full face—
demand that I pay attention,
all in one direction,
                    which would be,
ultimately,
all directions.
As it is, we say we make a choice.
I don't think it's that easy
or simple.
            What we say of it
is not the object itself.
Daily, this is what I look for, but
rarely find.
            Suddenly,
as if to help,
some sort of grand corrective,
the sun burns through the fog,
and my intimate view of the sea
becomes wider—
                    trawlers putting
in to South Bristol—
the outlines of the islands
coming clear again.
Yes, there is Allen's Island,
and my attention is shattered,
no,
        refracted
from many prisms in the lense.
Perhaps I'll make my way,
despite misgivings.

Listening for a sound,
all I hear is the ghost
of many sounds—nothing real.
The passion of the rain is only
a passion I set up

through whatever means I measure it.
(The rain now, on the keeper's skylight,
where he could look at night,
to see the beacon lit, or flaring,
in need of attention.)
The bell:
'Cast by Henry Hooper & Company, Boston, 1848.'
is some such ghost,
and reminiscent of its use, now useless/
voiceless—museum piece.
I'd rather be deafened in a fog.
Charter it to its use.
Its only use.

Later I see something of
'law of the sea and the interim,'
not a title,
                an actual place
for court action.
Well, the interim here fans out
to the sea.
                I stand
in that interim.
Whatever I make out of
wherever I stand—

that is the interim.
It is different from place.
It will not define as place,
stands up as will before the law.
It is from this that I prize it,
whatever its judge or being,
weight or color—
reprisals or blood sentence.
(Take that word—and that place as
touchstone.
                Finger it.)
Can't be certain
of what's clear—
each morning the sun tries,
and fails in a snow squall—
limps through the rest of it—
call it a day.

3/20/73
in a long period of
flurries

71

Or I might say something
of what I've called
ice clicks—
those small round counters
from a colder night,
and the stems, or roots,
or grasses bent over
dead into swift water—
early in spring.
early in fall.
Is it secretion like a pearl
from grit?
                    .where the stem
falls and stands still?
or does the water slow
to go around it?
Either one will do.
It's more through the joy
in seeing, early,
on a dull day.
That much comes clear from it.
Can't be certain
what I might say.
I go around the bend,
and the water lies
completely glass.
                    No ice.
It is good not to know
in such cases.
To marvel at it.
Pick up the straps
of whatever you're carrying,
and go on.

To think, as I did this afternoon,
of one word:
                    graveolens-
and to pick up further on it,
after some missteps—
ruta graveolens—
                    rue.
A substance from that dark plant
which may come to my hand—

a use,
though I do not know it now.
I am never far from such things—
thinking through them,
wondering what the other side
may bring—a use,
which is often a use
in pleasure—
that a thing exists—
something like ruta graveolens.

Pemaquid Point

Striae—as those rocks
upending the sea—
the end of the land,
or the sea, depending upon
where you stand—
or striae across the moon—
the high, thin cirrus—
news of another storm—
(end of the land—end of the sea.)

Here, it is nothing more than
going downstairs in the middle of the night
to load the stove again.
Warmth in the upper rooms,
deceptive,
            and cold creeps
next to the dying fire.
A simple thing, once known well,
now lost in the mystique of
'efficient' fuels—fossil
and artificial, and no heat
to bloom along the skin.
Few shiver in a windy house
at night—
or stoke a fire back to life.
(end of the land - end of the sea.)
Watching, yesterday, the knife edge
in the ice drift
finally drop away from the kitchen window,
apparently solid until
the last moment,
            as it slid

into the crevasse - honeycombed
below it—
            neat receptacle.
Hardly a thing of moment—
except that I made it so—
an interruption for other things.
Perhaps things more important?
I don't know.
It is not my place to order things—
merely to enjoy them—
moving through ice clicks, flurries,
striae of rock in surf,
clouds made and broken—
all of those things that make
a late winter
an early spring.
(end of the land - end of the sea.)
Watching and merely knowing
that it did happen—
that it was in place—
this place—that I
was my own part of it—
a part in ways
I couldn't tell you,
for all I might say of it—
do.
(end of the land - end of the sea.)

Well, I figured in for a little,
even as I helped the man
collect a few buckets of sap.
He looks for April snows,
wishes for them,
a help in his harvest.
All one to me.
The sap is here today,
may not be tomorrow.
(end of—
            what?
Congratulate myself a little,
but hope that I'm not more involved
than I can handle
at any one time.

That's the hell of it—
to attach and detach with equal grace,
so that nothing interrupts,
and all flows in easily,
or falls in a crevasse.
as if the pocket
had been made to hold it.
Don't be certain that it wasn't.
Not much by chance,
unless you destroy the real order,
which is in the laying of things
openly.
As one man says,
order, simply as one is able to find things.
Broken off—
        the bottle shard,
or bone spur—
sea rock—
whatever.
We go out and out to get at it—
sometimes do.
Often don't.
Compact this music out of sounds—
it is all music—
and I say it again:
MUSIC.
Not to interrupt—

XVI

'PI ZEEN! Aiiee!!
Pizeen!!!
      as I had it
from the old Portygee woman
who refused to go further,
dropped her cranberry scoop,
and pointed to the three leaflets—
poison ivy, trailing

through the cranberry vines
and red berries.
I couldn't blame her.
I had suffered so many times myself
from poisoning—
the anger of the skin—
outrage, which is the crux of it—
not rhus—works on us,
poisons.
Rage in the victim
is his death warrant.
'Aiyee! Pizeen!'
a warning chorus faintly
sounding,
                wafted,
fading,
            rising,
down the thread of history.
Whatever she said,
her agony sounding from it,
it was not her saying,
but consensus out of
all our saying—
graveyards and battlefields
full of it.
                (Times when we
didn't refuse,
and picked the fruit.

Often,
            late in the day,
shadows and clouds about equal,
I can't tell from a quick glance
if it's raining,
or something's beginnig to boil
on the stove—
                    (probably,
since it's near supper)
yes, I hear it more clearly now—
something boiling.
Followed by the call
from a friend

to announce his coming
tomorrow?
        (Must it be?
tomorrow?   Why tomorrow?)
But, as I said of interruption,
and that other land,
                Porlock,
I'll include him,
include his difference
with the sound of boiling,
and the rain,
if rain comes.
It's by this means
that I suffer a *good* digestion,
avoid pizeen.

Strange to remember it—
that time, and the old woman.
Thought little of it then,
and wondered who might venture—
greedy as I was for the berries.
Noting the darkness—
picking my way across
logs of treachery.
I spend my self learning
a few things at a time—
picking up seed—
prodigal cast.
(All of it won't flower—
what does,
cumbers the ground in places—
given a chance.)
Clear days and cold ones
build on the structure
of rain and warmth—
always—
        if it rains.
We fear most
what we do not have at the moment.
Building towards other roots—
or tearing down.

In my sense—
⎧teacher
⎨
⎩doctor
comes only
              (if at all)
at the end of life—
not learned in schools—
no credit - no degree.
The best teachers do not teach,
and what they know
is not experience.
An old man, from a new hand,
puts it down,
shapes it, as he plants a seed.
He will tell you, if you ask.
He will not begin the talk.
We learn to be chary
of what we say—
                    somewhat
because the breath grows short.
Somewhat because we are less confident.
'Diabolus in re.'
If we know (have known) pizeen
not much credit to us, if
we pass it on.
At times there is little else.
Not that what we know
outrages the skin and nerve,
but how we give it.
Does the ivy hate the man?
I doubt it.

To create this thing
out of my body—
maybe a different thing
than to comment on it?

Tension—
that coiled spring of the West,
mistaken for readiness,
unwinds and breaks back
to our hurt.
No sense of it

in true alertness—
as the cat
            ready to spring
relaxes.
When I look out—the new year
so fairly on,
there is a sense of looseness—
not slack—
The earth loosens her thighs
to bear.
Once more - once again.
Far cry from pizeen.
Nothing holds this day
but the element
in which it floats
preisely.

Cement on stone—
Why does that occur?
Why should I think of it?
What does it mean?
mean to me?
What holds the rock?
rooted like kelp
                or shell?
Why do I think of it?
What makes it clear purpose
to see in surf?
The tide-lock: thinking?
Thinking!
            But this is stone,
held to stone,
held to other things,
brother and friend,
enemy, and that which can't stay,
spends a moment there,
finds another level.
Is it that which holds,
or is held?
Space remains between.
Something passes through—
the other side,
which we think of

in terms of this one—
not the same thing.
Hard to pass by
this way.
                    Still, all in all,
made.
          A foot
step up
holding on rock:
Cement on stone.

Facets to surface—
the many surfaces rising
from what appears
a single plane.
I cannot move far
without climbing
or descending,
but I make do with this—
whatever I care for—
received as its own case.
Hardly a likeness,
but a way of being
                    like
the journey made
over the surface.
'Save the surface,
and you save all,'
Since what is outer
goes to the center,
peels back in levels,
and creates itself
as a totality.
Hardly making sense—
the density obscures—
swirls in its own fog—
but I am not hesitant—
can't go out far.
Cohesion to the surface—
'n you won't fall off.
The fears are useless.
Not much below—

but the slags
ores
of new surfaces.

All forms—in flowing
back,
the sense of danger,
and the sense of distance.
On such a morning,
rising to look out—
shaken.
The day in despair.
A day of death—

K.L. and as one dreams of death
so—one must die.
What happens in one dimension
balances the others—
though in ways not easily defined.
Moving through the eye of the day,
I go back to that hot afternoon—
the woman standing at the edge—
her whole self poised
in defiance—
not of anything alive
-malignant-
but the sense of poison—
how she knew it—
how she feared her own
outrage.
This from the surface—
hard to cull
or quell—
but of the surface
struck through to the center—
no seams—
no doors—
no apertures.
One does not sue
to any good-
appeal such wrath.
Step / aside.
Well, look out again,
see a day gone into seasons

we had left behind—
worry about that—
don't worry.
The outrage is in
the first attempt to challenge.
Challenge kills.
I hear that sound
grinding at myself.
Shading my eyes
against the falling light:
PI ZEEN!

XVII

Phlegethon—that flowing river—
because I make it so.
Thinking of it that way,
no time to go back,
revise or correct.
The flow is urgent—
                    found—
flow and flame.
                    Abrasive.
Active and whole-voiced.
Might be the original fire-flow,
a river of fire,
boiling stone down mountainsides
that cooled. Are looked on now
as dead—may reappear—
flow rock and ash again.
Nothing static—
                    and don't look back.
Loose arrows towards the source,
but over a shoulder,
                    with a mirror,
go on - downstream.
Do not forget: Carry the story,
our story, as the water carries.

Add.
Do not reverse except in tide.
But which direction is the flow?
Does it go in one place?
stemming from the shadow?
Fleeing it?
Into the eyes of darkness?
I don't know.
I pose a question.
Flow will carry - if the pulse
can find it.
We open up to that,
only in moments,
a form of love
given and accepted.

Those places where the cold
becomes its own head—
a cold river bursts with flame.
We do not see it warm
before we feel it,
scorched and honed,
flesh drops and we are light again.

Find her.
Find where she has been.
She is the fire
in this river,
though the river be a man.
She is in him.
Kenning for old songs—
old lines.
Reach her,
reach into her,
where her bowels smoke,
and the flame is hot
but raying out
touches the current—
starts in the river—
Phlegethon, my river,
my song of rivers,
source and mouth,
strait and bayou,

all that becomes
a river and a flame.
(Ourobourros turning,
flowing below low ground—
river muttering.)
Whenever I travel,
I travel by woman,
by her voice—
her movement
negating my thrust.

In simpleness look
to the meaning of myths,
do not read books for them.
What you will find there
has nothing to do with them.
They are absent.
It is not that fact.
Perhaps few facts are given.
Go out early in the morning,
pursed lips for smile—
do not forget to close the door.
Something gnawing
to get back in.
It is that time of morning—
sun breaking over clouds.
Wind rising—
a steel blue day
above cold water.
Antennae—
reaching toward the frost
or light—
perhaps the frost and light
themselves.
The blowing hair—
what we have called
the maenad's hair
once—
now- cloud—
which seems exact?
Spending these days—
that they spend us,
a joy and fear in that.

No way to come back—
no way to hold on.
A thin edge
moving over—
all that we have.
Not often thought of so:
Taken for granted—
and dropped.
Only for the hand
that might extend itself—
or the eye
behind itself.
(As the eye is closed,
the rest walks on.)
Walking in this place
where the houses are spread
so that you can see
from one to another,
rarely more than one
at a time.
And will not work its

fictive paralysis beyond
or around us.
How/what does that intrude?
portend?
Mean, if meaning is something
for the similar-centered?
What is the fear that betrays
as we go into darkness—
a stain reaching out from
the rug near the hearth,
into that darkness where
it becomes most real,
and most an argument of terms.
Suddenly the bright day
has shut in,
warm still, with a smothering
of clouds,
            to be followed
almost as suddenly by
cold/spring/rain.

Pick up the shards of another day,
go in
to admire them.
Look for something else—
tranquility or ease.

XVIII

What comes from the home place?
Enough wood to heat,
and cook whatever food
comes from it—
what one does and doesn't
plant there.
Every twig will start a fire—
'spriggin'' they used to call it,
and laughed. It was women's work,
but if the twigs were crooked
they'd fit around a pot.
o.k. and enough food to feed
a family of whatever it is.
The trip to town is for
extraordinary reasons.
What you need to live by,
you don't buy or bargain for.
How do you ask
for a service?
something you don't do
for yourself?
No further than a day's journey,
and that is by your own,
or a horse's legs.
If you don't believe this,
you have no right
to the home place
-in the first place-
and if it isn't large enough
to do this for you,

(if you're careful and use
all that's there—
use, not plunder,
and it's still not enough,
then you're in the wrong place,
or you have too much,
including children.
Malthus said something
about it,
he wasn't an authority,
simply pointed the way
through Anglican anxiety,
but
what comes from the home place?
enough to keep that place
and the people on it.
If you don't have that much,
then you are deprived.
I wish I could say
something else about it.
YOU ARE DEPRIVED!
When you sell
from what you think is surplus,
then you deprive yourself,
and there is no hope.
Better, that what you don't use
rots in a cellar
during late winter,
goes into the compost,
plant in it, the next year.
This is not popular talk—
an ecological means.
I will live with it,
and say something about it,
if I'm asked.

Late in the winter, we decided that the last of the pumpkins should be
used. A few of the seeds got taken with the rind to the compost heap. One
volunteer vine survived on all that pile of future life. The vine covered
approximately 2500 square feet, and produced fifty pumpkins before frost.

Whatever you buy
drains the sperm from your balls,

shrivels the ovum,
and you have no right to complain.
Cut and prune your progeny,
and find a home place.
If it ain't Ameriky,
then that was a wrong place
to begin with.
I have no solution.
I do know the problem.
That home place—
where,
within a day's walk,
a man can find
everything necessary
to heal sickness,
or a good place to die in.
Where a woman might
walk out and find rest—
where she might be alone
and bear her children.
Don't chide me.

Alonzo Shadman   A good doctor said the same:

"I have often said that a young woman would be far better off, and it would be safer, if on a summer day she could go off by herself, and lie down on green grass in the shade of a tree, and have her baby as Nature intended, not meddled with by anyone—"

And a man says
'but what if it *isn't* a
nice summer day,
and what if she hasn't the shade?'
We don't need the optimum
always,
                    and there are times
when it could be said
that withoiut these
                    home places
the ordinary things cut across.
We do not synthesize
except at peril
"But everything is synthesized now.
For fifty years or more

we haven't had a natural experience."
True,
            and it still applies.
Die back
            until you achieve,
or die in any direction—
this—without the place—
American dream—
                        technocracy—
including hard work,
whatever you want to call it, and do,
is not life.

Samuel Hahnemann   After the tailor dies
his customers are clothed.
Find what you want,
find at
one day's journey
still the best one
home and to one's bed.
Or extend it,
and lie where you have fallen,
where yoiu have gone
one day to the next.
You will,
            eventually,
go home.

XIX

George Johnston   What he said of all this:
That it must be basically story,
prepares me for argument,
not bristling,
nor in disagreement, exactly,
but for a defining of terms—
redefinition of what the story is.
As his story—
the fractured, wrenched fragments,

the dismembered spaces,
what passes outward
into the landscape—or in to us—
moves in—
the motif of all consciousness
(its notes)
to bring health—healing—
to make it roughly—
that way or not at all.
No loose ends
or knowledges.
(A gentle rain to lay the dust—
no more
   than that
it comes in showers,
stealthy, and at night—
this gentle, sudden rain
to lay the dust..)
We heard the music
and went out again.

Phocion of Athens Account of that man —so poor
that he must pay
his executioner for the sentence.
What news does *that* bring in?
That he borrowed 12 drachmae
for hemlock
says little more—
paraphrase of Demos- but that he cut the words
 thenes of Phocion of others to pieces
         says it.
A just man?
     I don't know—
a special pleading in his story
for something that strikes me
a cool morning in spring.
Note it down with other things—
a telling of his story—
the wonderment.
Put on any place to go—
find the placenta
and eat it—
all of this taken

out of hand—
mixture of the lie
and the lay of the land.
(Notation)
Where the tree fell,
an imprint
left from its branches,
a fan laid out
over the ground.
Story of the ascent—
of each year,
as the branches spread
to muffle the sun.
Is there anything more?
A story?
Has it ended there?
The man across,
busy shovelling snow,
under that tree,
has never seen it—
knows nothing—
perhaps heard it fall.
Huh?
Depends on the scarf,
where the scarf was laid,
ripeness of fall,
how fall made it.
And this is how the tree fell.

Fattened and ready to die,
none seem to think this,
lard in the belly,
more death waiting.

Book of Kells,
Image of St. Luke as a
calf

Figure of Luke—
I cannot forget it—
doing the best version,
merely by symbol.
Well,
        we'll have all of it.
The general in Athens,
paying for death,
learned a lesson early,

kept caution
as his stay.

Coming the proper way
around,
          one man
telling another of ways,
and what the sum means:
Civilized.
If that's what you want,
that's what you have
I suppose.
          Not old yet,
but I get tired—
stiff fingers in place
of a stiff cock.

Thinking of a wandering river,
one that changes course
abruptly—
          goes into
the sand and disappears,
rises again
          further on,
apparently from no source,
because it is hard to follow
or connect with sources.
The wonder of history,
or why it should interest me
that a man in Athens
paid for official hemlock
          and drank it.

Finding out the height
of any mountain—
cut through,
          not mere triangulation.
Not timberline—
the high outcroppings
East Hampton, Mass.   stab and frown
above the bottom lands—
that simple
          that height

is the same reason
he drank
       (what he paid for.)
If you don't like this,
or labor with non sequitur,
let me twist your head
a little
       to look in there.
The simple place
where the view falls *in* place—
your place
       no one else
sees it that way.
       Story
or history,
       blind magic.

Meant to stay longer
with it—
       dare not.
I walk the dust
out treading
       sea
oh tides—. .

XX

Faint odor   crushed ferns
a good smell in early spring—
so few   thin air to carry
scent and cold.
Hard bitten, I'll stay well
as any bud
       wormed up
in bitter weather,
to the taste of galls.
It is my nature so
and to remain this side of water
with the ferns.

As if the ground would rust—
rot /
     / out—
the seven days of rain
forecast by wise men
has come to us,
and been surpassed.
I would go, if there were choice,
to the *far* side of water.

What does a man think of?
turned in upon himself?
in rain?
        how keep the verdigris
from choking?
             as it spreads
across his roofs?
sours his ground.
Not to escape, this history,
nor to ensure the same mistakes.
Looks at it as a live thing,
perhaps the only life
in shadow of the flood.

I am too tired
             to write any of this
clearly—or without feelings
anchored in mist.
The night is a cold one,
I   choose my way.

"The rain, if it last too long
in spring—
        dispirited,
as it dispirits us."

These crushed ferns, now,
by the outlet of the spring—
another spring
          eternal,
as that hope which springs.
Finite. And that one
          must be.

Still, I remember the old man
whom I met on cool spring mornings.
All around us, fresh.
He said, invariably,
if I asked him how he was,
"Tired, young man.
                    Tired."

An agonizing rain,
as self-deception—
agony of the man—
this man—or any—
sodden, where the spring is sodden.
Tired—
            young or old man.
What has come to pass?
What pass is this?
The interminable fog and mist
rot
    what the rain pierces.
And I sit here recalling
a tired old man, as if
that were more important,
as if it held a moment,
the secret of history,
or what may be gleaned there—
put to use.
Better to turn back
to the crushed ferns,
sensing their place in it—
running from that sense
no matter how much rain,
or how many old men are tired.
a slow day—
credited to others—
well,
            tomorrow we'll give her hell.

Bitter days—
the days of waiting.
A man looks out,
sees sun on water.
The morning catches him,

holds him gently,
as if in its hand—
by noon—high clouds,
before supper,
                    rain again.
He goes to bed fearful
and without hope.
Each day made in the same shape,
and his boots grow tight
from water.
His flesh, and his soul
shrink.

Few ways out of it—
though we go, eventually,
comparing this year to others—.
"In the year of '78—
again in '03.' Maybe he learns something—
a way to plant crops :
'Wait until the ground's bullin''.
An eye to moon phase—
the last frosts.

I can think of all of it,
squatting on my hocks.
Crushing / a / few / early / ferns /

C.T. Hodgkins

XXI

Again and again
the connections.
There is no absolute
                    center.
The core of the earth shifts,
and I see the centering
of parts.
        I move away
to see this one
                centered—

hold it in my hand.
                              I know the fit,
not yet the place.
                              I cannot rise
to it - and yet I do.
                              All these
voices centered in my ears—
Their words.
                    What have they said
to me ?
          The clarity is there,
but not in voices.
                    Simply there.
I cannot substitute one thing
                              for another.
I do not give up
                one loyalty
to find another.
I am not split
                nor torn,
hardly unhappy.
                    No division.
the simple joy
                comes through
complex things—
                    rounds out
a life.   His story.

You gave me sun and water.
I cannot refuse them.
I spent some time in
                    question,
about them,
                then realized
I had gone beside the point—
that I accept, as you do,
the facts.
          And if we do,
there is no transgression.
It is not bidden to come or go.
It is here,
          and that is that.

Order of impressions by which
I give / receive a love
in purity.
        One must reform
each —
        anew—
the songs of morning.
Sun   water   light.

Post coitus tristum est.
All right,
        I apologize for Latin,
but the sense is there.
             Implicit.
Realized.
        It is not sadness,
but that quiet which precedes
             sleep
after fucking.
        At that point
I can take your center and live within it—
know that there are other centers—
business which concerns me—in which
             I live, -
and that I live so singly
           - comes from
multiplicity.

        I would consider
your body, lying beside,
           over or under
mine.   The waking there,
          and what we felt
in waking.   Not that it is different
from the experience of others—
but that it links us to them—
many centers
        centered fully.
It is not the first or last
           of it.

What else is there to say ?

Casting the I Ching
                  we found
a base—
           that the superior man
lives at limits,
              but within them.
Which is to say :
              A recognition
of those many centers—
                  makes a use of them.
Sun   water   light.

Touch or no touch—
always the connections,
fully realized into love.
The trickery of thinking
attempts to turn things around.
Oh,
        what I would try with you.
That is a fiction.
              Simply in these close acts,
concern.
And they are close at any center.
Pay attention, and you will not
go wrong.
          Why do I expand it ?
For no reason other
than that of my / his story
put into context,
and that means,
sun   water   light.

A bath in elements—
the rich savor of them.
Things we cannot reach beyond.
What will others make of this ?
I can't tell,
            nor is it important.
I go my way
            with or without.
I am not deprived—
whatever deprivation means.
I am engaged.

The years I did without,
willfully,
listening to other voices
than the one within.
All that is past,
and must be.
Wondering is wandering.
The concern is center.
That is all we have to move from.
Out and in
as if
it were the pulse:
lunar and solar—
tide of land and sea.
I go high on this,
will not come down.
Loves find their levels.
We will find our own—
the connections measured in:
Sun   water   light.

XXII

Lies open to question,
so long as the question is open,
draws on the blood.
Wince of pain—not mine—
the faceless
struggling for an audience.
I give it, but am not convinced.
What might I say to them?
It is not clean-edged.
Only their wills:
praise of manifest
destiny.
The only thing we haven't got.
Lived on in that illusion.

Built in facades which reflect
                              folly.
And it comes to feeling.
One feels as one does,
not as one wills.
                    It is not brave
to attempt to put out fires,
or shore up ruins.
                    Get the hell out—
out of the way, amd let the dead
mature to dust.
                    Squeaking of bats.
The attempt to hold on.
                    Ash heaps
grow.
          We are embedded there.
And the outlet—
the sense of where
one might be saying
what one was saying—
was it?
          Aphasia
it seemed to be—
                              was
somewhere else.
I spent time enough on this.
Perhaps I thought
of distance
                    as mere mileage?
Something came down,
quickly spent itself.
Like the final come—
one slips off
                    flaccid
to sleep.
                    Hardly a murmur
over breathing.
                              (stertorous cough.
Is she sleeping?
Do I disturb anyone
at late rounds?
Making a peace from it—

a justness
             or is it
a quality—
something opaque?
Dependent on its own sense
to make clarity
                of weight?
I spent more time
                than I know—
a harbor of guilt
to the source
from the outlet.

I must see these
living forms of flesh
alone
        apart
from where I set myself—
the outlet and
                the inlet
close enough
                and by
my standing
                by - enough
to see
        and gone.
I place my hands
across my eyes.
Well, sense it out—
let us be gone.
Whatever made
was gone
enough to say
no simple thing enough.
The flesh remembered
                        then,
to sound
        and darkness—
falls apart.

What then,
                do we think of clarity?
looking back?

                              No,

G.O.

                    we do not think of it
                    in that man's terms.
                    He said it,
                    and there is no
                                        mistaking
                    or interpretation.
                    A man who spent his life
                    centered—
                                        possibly mistaking
                    the many for the one.
                    But he took it.
                                        Held it
                    in his hands—
                                        opened his heart—
                    a full flood.
                    Opening to the point
                    where I would send him roses,
                    but not such roses
                    as are grown.
                    Let me think,
                                        but with my hands—
                    my toes in earth.
                    It is there his story
                                        rises
                    or arises.
                                        It is clear.
                    Few days we spend
                    such places,
                                        where the wind
                    takes off from skin.
                    There is no division,
                    and the question rises
                    where the lake imposes
                    shores.
                    Do we know
                                        where the land ends?
                    I have asked these questions
                    of myself.
                                        Received no answers.
                    But there are no answers
                    ever.

Simply questions.
If we look for clarity,
we ask.
There is nothing,
                    no one,
who will answer.

Who speaks of heart's dismay
speaks well,
                    comes from the end
to what can center.
                         I reach
the top of such a wall,
and so,
          come down.
The drop is there.
I rose one morning
                      to it.
Drawn up as tight
                      as briefs in law—
what one may know
of walls or rising,
heart's blood sticky
in a drying sun.
Corpse and fetish
in a land of deserts—
sharp peaks
                that wound
a landscape.
                  Salt
and crystal
                faceted.

Hard country.
                    and a man
drops out to death
as easily
              as another breathes.
Well—
          take me to to such mountains.
The dry echo
—falling stones—
is part and counterpart

of story.
In part we know it—
part is fear.
the touch, a graceful arc
outside,
      and no one
stays there.

All of this moonlight
gathered in a small room—
but at the full
the power's lost—
even on a tide
of light -
      reflection—
sent out
      and over again.
It disappears day by day,
poses the question,
and no heat.
I rise from madness
into
   other
madness.
Complication of the web—
it arches
     over me.
It breaks the blossoming—
perhaps
     nothing
but a shatter of old petals
dropped in sleeping grass.
What can anyone say?
Why should anyone try?
Questions.
Questions become the hum of insects—
crickets and cicadas
on a still, late summer's night.
Followed by questioning eye:
          the sun
in mists and heat—
a question of the morning.

The red and gold united—
heat, and a day for sweat.
Break out of it.
I must complete the span
in shorter time
                    than these
I know.
Talking late at night—
the febrile excitement
carries across to this
vague day in summer.
Only a few things clear—
the question of love again,
occluded in some places,
but a certainty.
No one to ask—
and little bread among the stones.
Pushing that limit,
but holding to its shape.
I take this heart as
heart indeed.
Perhaps it was bidden
in a place a
                    biding,
which is to stay there.
Shake like an old dog,
pass on /
            / proceed.

I will not look to find it
in what is common
                        or uncommon.
I will not look to find it,
and if I find
            in looking,
by the look
            it may have been
closed smile
            or openness
I have never found
                    hiding a stone—
which may be smile and look—
that pivot

where I reach
or try to touch
            the center.
Blame or blameless. Saintliness—
that blasphemy has reached
                    this morning.
I must go my way—
                and look
                    or not.

Now reason and the question—
where they crowd
could make such opening.
The field of flowers,
                coreopsis:
bug-eyed one,
            or maiden's eye—
misreading,
        as I see, yes,
maiden's eye. Do not disturb mistakes.
I read it right,
and there I found
the spate of questions.

XXIII

How much?
            How much to know?
I'd take it from the orator.
Not what the man said,
but how he stood,
                where he
said—
        to stand / withstand.
(And those who stand do not
with
    stand
            but alone—
always to sea in an open boat.

How much?
How much to know?
Complain?
the drove of bees—
hot summer's day.

And all this time
long talks,
with talking out,
few things to dare—
come back to.
What do I touch?
Who holds the skein?
Must close myself against
the day,
must walk
to climb the blaze of night—
blue shadow
from behind.
What do we hold?
and when we hold,
is part of that the hope
that somewhere the land
will relax—
the muscle weaken—
and the hold
drop?
More than likely,
and it is the place where
reasons fall.
If I have reason
good or not
to do anything
I had best not
do it.
It is only in impingement,
when the head and heart
and hand are all at one
in one strict place,
answering only as they come in contact.
I have found that only once,
which might say
that I have had one moment granted me:

Life.
And this is not denial.
I have been denied
                    only what
I denied myself.

Symposium of madness
What do I ask the orator?
Why do I talk to him?
He is the orator—
my voice is less than his—
skims off into the moonlight—
that terrible shine—
waking me—
                    -past midnight—
that I rise into it—
pitiless eye—
a place to wade—
a place to
            look
for shadows.
Are there none?
No reprieve?
I see the tree,
and I see that moon caught
in its branches.
No reflection
but that reflected light.
These nights before the full,
and how the full is useless
there—
            the nights of wax
I Ching   are those of power.
Use them wisely.
Be used by them.
And I am struck full face—
this clarity—
which I lack.
At this point, I am outside it.
Pray to return.

It is that clarity which surpasses
greatness.

Mistaken for stature,
it is only clarity.
One must not accept homage
for such a thing.
It is lost at that moment,
and a man's voice
                    dies away.

In past ten years,
the moon
            so many times at
waning point—
                    in perigee and apogee
one hundred twenty cycles—
                                        that
point again.
                I see and
hear it
            echo in reflection—
is a sense so charged
it passes here,
from one to another.
I am sitting,
                strangely quiet,
and the light goes out.
And in these past ten years,
so many times the ache
that follows in fulfillment.
I had thought I finished there,
and left to history
those moments—
                    ***
                        Now the pitch
of moonlight
                angled to this bed,
that climbs its outline,
traces where she lies
-her hips and breasts-
her sleeping face.
Those eyes asleep.   —
Goes on
            to me.

Red Jacket

A madness and a fever—
such hard things.
Places that we dream of—
that orator who might have shared.
Our voice
              has gone away.
Those tribes whose records
kept in voices
                    gone
in shadows.
              Only this—
our bed and moonlight.
Where we come together—
as the common ground—
we have few things
                    'in common'
save ourselves.
              But that is absolute.
We will make love again.

This time the door has opened.
We are taken through—.
Ourselves, and,
what we know of selves.

Well, you have asked me
to tell you
              a ghost story.
I will begin.
We will not forget.

XXIV

My love
        (my loves)
I have something to teach you:
We have thought
                    it comes easy
to love,

and have worked
that direction
                looking at
what we have held
                as
what we are holding?
                        no, a
thinking that ease comes of
compromise /
                / accomodation.
Perhaps it's a way,
but none that I follow, or care to.
Look.
        If I choose you,
                        I
choose, and no other.
I will not, in marriage,
take more than yourself.
I take heed of your lineage,
but I take you away from the coast
and across rough seas.
You will not see your father
                                again,
nor your mother.
                They do not come
this way.
                They, too,
must mature,
                grieve, but let go,
as we all.
                All of the bones
that we stand on—
                        free—are
alone,
        though they link on
to another
                one dust
to another - drier.
                        Go down there
in kinship— come up as yourself.
There is nothing to fear
                                except
what is afraid in one's self.

Keep what is kept
                    for your children.
The old must let go.
                         Look again.
They would like to hold you
with papers,
                    legalities,
monies-:
          that you must
come home for a Sunday dinner.
No!
     You will break yourself.
It is not love to go home again—
even for the funeral.
Unfortunate respect.
                    Drop it!
Come out as yourself.
                    Only then
that you come to your children—
give to them—
                    and let go in your turn.
A usury by such as hold coin.
Death to them—
                    not even wished:
they have death in their veins.
They rot to bequeath it.

Do you remember?
                    A story once told
is a part of it.
                    The young man
stands by the side of his father
in flood time—
                    and his son stands
with him.
          The flood is too much
for the old man—
                    too much for the child.
The young man takes his son—
says goodbye to his father.
The father, a wise man,
blesses him,
          says,

"Yes, and well done.
                    I would have chosen
as you do."
               Listen, my love,
and do likewise.
                    I can respect,
but I do not walk under past shadows.
I see the poised rocks,
                         and your danger.
Do you?
          See it?
(Not that I take you
                    imposed.)
Do not listen to those elder traditions—
unless you live where they apply.
This is experience wrenched
from its context.
                    This kills.
Come into life,
                and come equal.

It is not that I ask of you
more than I ask of myself.
It is easier to look back
than to look where there is nothing—
known or unknown.
                    Reefs and a fog,
no buoys - no lights - no bells.
Perhaps I congratulate strength
which I do not have.
                    I have staked the lot,
and the lot may
                easily
be lost.
          But I do go on—
pegging at quandary,
                      asking no help
in such times of division.
                         I am saying simply
in light of our coming,
                       in light of all
  coming.

Will you, alone,
out of yourself,
                come?

There is space for our rushlight—
our doors—
                beyond dangerous waters.

XXV

Not a misconception—
                a cruel man—
conquistador.
                And that's not all of it.
By his own lights, just.
Upright in matters of religion—
what he thought he could bring
in return for the gold he thought they had.
Came through the chapparal—
                cactus and mescal,
burning with thirst and with avarice—
somehow always in debt.

From that:
                (Fortuitous / ominous
drop of the windfall /
                water / fall /
wood—one stick on the inner island—
the night before frost.
                Make haste.
Haste.)

Into Tenochtitlan—
                that sorry business—
bringing death,
                destruction.
Losing what must not be lost.
And *that* is my / his story.
What is lost.

115

How it is lost—
loosed to the winds.
(Malinche, Malinche,
you have loved too well.)

(Pick up the stick.
                    Cut it off—
fitted for the fire—night fire.
One you may not use,
warmed by drink and good talk.)

How long he went through back country—
ill—
        -more-
ill at east.
                He did not want to
destroy the image he had:
One he held of himself.
"Your gracious majesty,
I am in need."
"I feel sure your majesty will
understand the situation,
                            and send-"
Most of it to deaf ears,
if any were turned that way.
Ships laden with treasure,
lost along the Main—
                        a beginning
for such fortune.

(Sitting and wondering
if this will be the night—
one night of frost
to plough another year
                        under.
Possibly.
            Or will a wind?
A few clouds?
                later?
Give new lease?

(And,
    as those flowers
followed back—

                    the helianthus
                              sun flower
          setting its head towards light—
          anxious for it—
          droops on a dull day—
          looking west—
                              was that where?
          The cities of Cibola?
          Only, as a simple flower,
          single—
          seed dropped by winter bird.
          Or such as corn—
          one stalk beside the road,
          untended—
                              but allowed.
          A magic seed.
                              perhaps
Teachings of Don   One that lost its magic,
    Juan   and grew tall.
          Age for it,
                    withering.
          The winter comes on now and
          blackens it.
          Showers.
          Rust shivers in the evening breeze.
          It smites mine eyes.)

          "And I beseech your majesty
          to look kindly on these small things
          sent you,
                    as in course,
          "that which is your majesty's due."

Cortes: Fifth letter
    to Charles V,

        "Then, during Muteczuma's lifetime all the gold that was obtained
in the capital was melted down and a fifth sent to your Majesty, which
amounted to over 30,000 castellanos; and although the jewels would also
normally have been divided up, each man receiving his share, yet both they
and I gladly decided not to distribute them but to send them all to your
Majesty, to the value of over 500,000 pesos."

ibid.   "But I maintain that such gold as has been obtained has not been sufficient to prevent my remaining a poor man and in debt to the tune of over 500,000 pesos of gold without so much as a castellano with which to pay it."

> Rapine and plunder do not
> enrich a man for long.
> He stands in the dry desert wind,
> despairing of a draught of wine—
> even
> > of good water.

And yet another time:

Cortes' triumphal land
ing at Palos, May 1528.

His train was magnificent: native princes followed him, vaulters, jugglers, dwarfs; there were wild birds and animals, tigers, lions, pelicans. "a great store of coaks of feathers and skins, shields, featherwork, mirrors of polished stone, and many other things of like nature, including treasure in gold and jewels to the value of some 300,000 pesos."

> (Under my heart the spell—
> the promise of new birth.
> This death is transient—
> do not say
> all things are.
> I move to see the rain
> as seed.
> > I see it:
> as it puts down
> > > life
> into the earth—
> each pockmark frozen
> is a place for living;
> under my heart—oh
> in
> > and under
> > > over
> out - around—
> > > the spell.
> Let not the demons touch
> or take.
> > Keep from me

118

Take over
           to where the night becalms.
The new moon,
cusp of the elder—
lust
        on.)

    Haniel Long:
Malinche (Dona Marina)
"She who speaks to you.

    "When my father the Cacique of Oluta died, I being eight years, my mother sold me to Tabascan slave traders to rescue the inheritance for my half brother."   — "that Malinche whom Hernan Cortes called Marina."

    "I rise and begin dancing without knowing why."

    "Love is teaching me his language quickly."

    "This is a lover who will not age, who will need to wait ages to give you all of himself."

    "For support I fall back on my heart. Has a man any fault a woman cannot weave and try to change into something better, if the god her man prays to is a mother holding a baby?"

    "He is really afraid that Cortes may prove to be Quetzalcoatl."

    "—under my heart the child of Cortes."

    'And I shall bear my lord his babe."

So that,
        some of those conquered eventually called Cortes himself, 'Malinche.'

    "Cortes returned at the beginning of June in 1526 to find the country more or less at peace. His triumphant journey from Vera Cruz to the capital was lined with eager throngs of natives: they cried out 'Malinche, Malinche': tears of joy streamed from their eyes. There could have been no more eloquent testimony to the misgovernment of the country during his long absence."

119

sign of hare or rabbit.
Take strength in bull's horn,
sanctuary in the wheat—
new mown and broken—
threshed and flailed.
The barn floor new and scrubbed.
Water of the sun through cold clouds.
The dance, now slow,
becomes the heat of night.
Oh child,
                    under my heart.

Was it a lie?
                    Did he suffer that much?
I would ask such questions,
but I might not know such answers.
He looked on mountains—
The smoking mountain and
the white woman—
those which were husband and wife,
and he knew,
somewhat as those others,
grace, which is in all religion.
Cruelty.
                    To pluck the heart out.

Whom he referred to
                    only as:
"a native Indian girl—"
the thread—
interpreter.
Who bore him several children,
supplanted those wives—
wenches and whores in Spain,
or in houses of governors:
Malinal
Marina, as she was baptized.
Malinche.
All of them,
                    all wives
from the sea.
(And there is little left to say,
except that blossoms crushed

Popocatapetl and
Ixtaccihuatl

120

in the fall make
the best wine—
clear as a thin sky—
pale—
cold for the new year.
Listen to what I would say,
but do not follow.
The year rots out,
if it is heeded.

XXVI

Landnamabok

As place becomes:
The book of lands and names,
of naming, and the boundaries
fixed on this—

               unfixed before—
the wind

           eternal wind.
Few trees except in sheltered valleys—
the dales.

       So is a unity
made for things dispersed
diverse—

      as may be
personal / impersonal,
relevant — im-

           pertinent.
this is

    His / my story:
SELAH.

That this man held his lands,
or granted some of them
to another—

        son or freedman,
makers of its histories—
the markers—

lists and catalogs
                    for example—
of rights—riparian,
the summer sheiling,
all such recounted.
What is the use of it?

Ah,
        but I have no high seat.
As the seat becomes high.
House pillars cast into the sea
came to these shores—
abandoned.
There is no one else here.
I will set my house
upon the rocks,
on shores that no one knew
except those few
who left bells and script.
I will worship   Thor—
or at the fanes?
what makes a difference.
We are high men
so long as we don't think we are.
Worship:
Thor or Odin?
or the land itself?
That is it—
the place of land and names—
a good place for sheep—
grasslands.
Riparian rights—
and the sea—
                    the sea always.
the place for ships—
men and whales—
my god—whomever my god—
a place for going,
as the women sit at home
and tend.
            As here, and daily,
I dredge up from gardens
remembrance of other days—

brass rings
          and marbles—
ends of things—
their human element.

Standing again at streams, I look
and see the shadows—
wine red—
          the wine of fall
comes down—
               the maples turning,
and the end of all the years.
My wine-red stream,
or some dilution of old blood.
I look and think,
turn back to where my high seat
might have stood—
a hole in time—
a mute encircling—
center of the storm
where all is quiet.
Out of the lips that are dead/
not dead—
          the center
of the storm—
          all quiet.
Out of the self that is living/
not live,
     all quiet.
Cover with compost—
leave through the fall
and the winter—
               come back
back
     all quiet
to spring.

"And during that winter,
all was quiet."
regenerate.

How does place become?
over this hill?

that one in fall—
north, and so
                    early.
I walked down a little way
thinking of names,
of naming,
                    and a book of names,
a field of bones.
I lived my life there.
Out of the canker and the sore,
I rose and came up—
                            came back.
Yes, yes I will stay.

                    XXVII

So,
        I took that time—
(time which I did not have)
and watched from the morning,
how they
                    put together
                                the tents,
and set up the booths,
and waited under the mountains
until men came
                    to buy—
to be cheated,
                    knowingly,
but to be there together
in noise and confusion
before the shadows came down
from the mountains,
                            and the snow
swept the fields.
                            I was one
of them - emptying my pockets—
my heart to such men

as I never saw elsewhere,
                                    once
a year,
            on that field
in the mountains,
                        woods close—
a good place.
                        A place for the prize.

North New Portland
Fair

I spent time—strength—
                        far more
than the money.
(Thinking at this point—
no woman ready for no man—
unless she forsake,
                        and he forsake,
that they produce together
a union in obeissance to themselves.
That they:
forget the past—
live from it,
            out of it.
Do not despise it,
yet know that children are not beholden—
are free from parents.
Kiss and farewell.)

And on those grounds,
the hawkers/
                /barkers/
men with fried food,
women at gaming tables:
"All right, folks,
                step right up."
"Every game a prize."
"Everyone wins."
"Who's next?"
They did.
            They bit.
No sense of order in it.
Take that later
                after
ferris wheels,

French fries,
plaster ducks.
Squash and apples,
pickles and aprons.
The pull
       and the teams
in the rain.
          Ending.
Come back tomorrow.

(Trying to make sense
out of life
lived in strange places,
improbably unions.
Who is alive?
Who pays the debt?
Is something owed?
In what specie?
You?
Who do you think you are?
To anyone—most yourself?
Lust and false coin.
Someone said of it—
some
     thing

And in full swing
another day—
the horses and men—
the old ones,
         young ones,
balloons torn away
          upward—
sun on the mountains.
Young men,
      old women.
The tired girls dancing—
odor of crotch,
       and the sad men
watching.
      One sang me his version:
"Big Rock Candy mountains."
What do they know?

Well, what can they sell?
Why bother?
Goodbye—and torn paper—
go on to the outside.
Wondering
            air and smoke.
The crowd breaks away,
houses wink on
                        cold.
Lights in the villages.
Late supper.
                  I tell you,
Mr. Man,
            fairs ain't what
they was.
                  But this'll do."
(Cry to the women—
the past and *that* cry—
that the close things
are hard ones to deal
and deal with.
Crystal and amethyst.
Coming to leaves now—
leaves for the winter.
Down - all down-
Set up shop.

XXVIII

'Everyman's right,'
a right to pasturage.
Not merely the
                  citizen—
any man on passing through,
who camps:
            Sea islands,
or among the rocks.

'A string to the right
                    or
the left of the arrow.'
Bolt—or sheet lightning—
enough to touch the rock—
shaft / let / go.

(Do we live with ideals ?
Do they become other
in reality ?
            My love, my love,
in whom such sense of it.)

And if the tent is pitched
on land worked over,
arrows working loose
may rise to touch—
and sink again.
We use what has been used.
There is no thing
that cleaves to men.
I tense in spirit,
break from past,
but am the past.
Come with me,
we will place it
here or there.

Looking through
to that seat of power,
what one knows,
and how one cares for it.
The urge and demiurge—
what moves.
Is it the story ?
or the fact ?
at what point my story
becomes the real
and loses consciousness ?
There were many times,
days to think of it.
Sitting alone in the house
by the cornfield,

Lamont, Michigan

128

waiting for her to come.
Did I think of *her*?
or was it merely in her being
that I did?
        became her,
the her as hers,
and not foreseen.
Our idea?
The power is more
within the cornstalks,
between them,
given to the wind,
and I drive on.

My love,
        the strength of this
my portion given.
And salts of night
that flow together.
Each and every man.
his right - the due
once given
        once
imposed.

Things unspoken
showering a landscape,
the arrows bright
and centered—
oh
the day of arrows—
how one feels—
and where one goes
with them.
I do not know.
        I cannot come—
less and loose.
The loosing of a way—.
What I recoup?
No, where I walk,
as tending,
        how I know
and ask to travel.

Symbols do not do it.
It is in the real,
and that is all that says—
is said—
                his story opens
broken open,
                        milk and meat.
Intoxication of the flesh—
is all that these—
                        reminds me—
certain air—.
Break off—
                the fire
touches me—
                        and things more real
in burning ruins.

One will ask me,
"Just what is the situation,
                                now?"
I can't tell.
                I try to—
hortatory in this absence,
and the last days
                        sitting
where I may not sit again.
Well, I'll square the circle,
hold the cube,
                        extend
and say it—
                all of it—
more clearly than the hope.
We will,
                we will arise,
know darkness—
                        touch on fate,
and how the flow of blood
depends on anger.
Simple things—
                        the look's delight.
I had no care for it before.
A ground glass
                        broken underfoot—

but more than shatter.
Take my hands—
                    each one is warm.
But warmth can mean
so many things—and other
loosed on plain
and in the mountains.
(How they breathe:
One breath for day and night.)

(To reach
          be there
before it begins—
of storms
          of lives.)

(To be aware of what's around
the only form
                of wisdom.
Maxims.
          May be.
Treading for the water hole—
spring at the head
                    of the draw,
as it becomes
the head of the dream—
the opening
          out
of the close
          under
wide sky.

To be alive,
          as it happens,
not alone,
          the woman sleeping
in the house,
          and I am
waking—
          that as good fortune,
when I return
          again.
As so it seems to be

nostalgia
                out of life
and into it—
                        from what
the history might be.
Move on—
                the eye at level
over
        wavering
the land.

Whatever the sense of land,
There are people on it,
and in it.
                Place is only good place
as one knows this—
its emptiness
                        presupposes,
prefaces
                the long march
in.
        Nostalgia
for his / story?
A pinch of dust
followed by a spatter
of rain with snow.
High wind
that rocks the land,
subsides in cold.
What is it all about?
Why should it be?
an opening—
                and a close.
Full stop.

Leading by fortune
back to that night.

Around here,
                after the cold wind passed,
I pitched my tent.

Hanna, Wyoming

XXIX

Higher than mountains—
perhaps for doing,
(and in the air
                    are mountains—
wedged and broken
                        I have found
a way over,
            under crevasse,
to the edge of the air,
                        and the question:
"What have we left out?
                        What is undone?"
I make my way further,
thinking:
            Thinkng only
of the talk—
                talk of despair,
but no despair in it.

In time of fear,
                    a place for fearing,
a good fleece
                cut off in its prime.
Delilah, shear me?
                    not at all.
The way in or out of strength.

(Years ago,
                years
alone
        and drunk and lost,
at twilight near those houses—
misfortune
                in a neighborhood
I didn't know—
a town I did.
How did I fare?
and how come through?
I am sitting here
                now,

Chatham, Mass.

133

quiet, if unsettled.
Safe, if cold.)

And
    as a wise man said,
"The best that I have ever done,
is live with Helen."
Would to say that,
               · if I could.
As the chance lay open.
That I too know
a woman—beautiful—
with whom—with whom—
from every cave
the body holds—
go in, go out,
and be
    strong sunlight
pure water
      place
or fortune
      know the act.
The primal lore—
the logic's
    hiatus,
which is logic—
is the space of it—
the love, the story,
hers and mine.
No dream of love.
The act itself
speaks solid as an oak,
secure in future of its kind.
Well,
    whatever saying,
I would live with her.
            Higher than mountains ?
Perhaps the buzzard flies there
in this jackal winter—
something unkind
      no more than death
spread on the snow,
that melts and cringes

under unsettling winds and skies.
I have walked through it.
I have talked to it,
cursed myself,
                    and
wondered
            solely because
there was nothing else to do.
Quite simply,
                no matter what the risks,
I would live with this—
                    with her.

Now, from others
I get a sense of it:
That they do not like me,
nor my choice,
                    precarious,
some of it, perhaps,
but they are thinking in their own terms.
Well, that's possible.
Let them.
            I have work to do,
places to go,
and I may yet go alone.
It is hard to fix on men—
stay with them.
Cursed by them.
Higher than mountains.
That would be the emblem.

One who takes photographs.
He did not—
was it the company I kept?
This one looks for letters—
thinks I have hidden them,
surprised at how easy it is
to find what I did not hide,
but put out of common reach,
which is common harm.
It is a world where I do not
laugh or cry.
I do not know that I like

my sense of it—
much less yours,
Higher than mountains?
Ptaah!!

Still, I will go out
on a warm still morning,
walk and let the sun
lie heavy on my skin.
It is a place for it,
and I within the place.
Do not take the place
for men within the place.
I have never had
what I have not wanted
at a particular time,
but later, with other tools
at hand
I have gone away in disgust.

Something a man might learn,
but it is doubtful.
He will not.
Something that happens:
Recurs - is
         re-
current.
       Open as a shaft
laid to the sunrise.
Nothing there I want,
nothing is possible.
Wind - wind—
always the bitter scream—
and move the stiff cheek
of a cold rock
lying beneath it.
Flexing myself —able
but unwilling—ready
to pick up tools
and go on.
There is no stopping it.
Once we are born

there is death
             ahead
no matter or sense
to the wind between
a void in events—
a voidance.
Dance out the changes.
Good luck.
             You will need it.
A coin beneath
the stepping of the mast.
Set sail on it.
Whatever crowding
might be for us,
there is darkness
and whirlpool—
the voidance of water.
I tempted myself
once in that pleasure—
the opening ridges—
the pleasures of mountains.
The valleys between them.

XXX

In route of doing
what is rout?
What makes?
What is the root,
and what is loss?
should it be
             loess?
How many times
to cover up what was—
is not
      was
made - was -
well - how does one sing?

Why should one?
What are precepts.
What are questions?
Not to void, but leave
the answers
to those who cannot ask
the questions?
Well, and how, what place—
where did one live?
Is that the house
'of wattles made'?
or is it of stone
that does not endure.
Look you, it falls,
and forms in land
or ice or water
in its season.
Let one sin
for such blind joy,
the joy in singing,
that will cure, and will ease
the heart in curing
where the heart is—
where mating birds—
that early mating—
                          come.
Chaucer knew of it.
Why cite dead poets?
if they are live,
they do not live by books
or stones
commemorative?
Oh the casket,
or a first day stop.
Let me know,
and let me out of this.
I pushed somewhat,
and then fell back.
Come mystery.
I am
      choked with sound,
will set some here

Charles Olson

to come alive—
if someone finds it—
or even wants it.
Making in some crumpled way
a history or motion
towards me,
if they do—
what risk?
And why should misplaced papers,
misapplied
make more than one shrug
off the shoulder
at the moon?
At least I said
'at' and not 'upon',
not wishing to go there,
or to bring back
dust and stone
of afterbirth.
The drunken step,
also, mayhap the slip,
and some old swords
with new ones,.
set them next.
All lonely men
have spent their mornings
in by fires,
against a bitter wind—
the chill—
why factor it?
It's cold!
I spent more time than most
in standing
gloating at my store,
which shrank the moment
I had looked at it.
What fires?
Is this the time
for hankering?
or hunkered down,
why should I think?
All prisons make

of what is made—
the thought comes later,
if at all.

And what I meant:
a file in someone's bread,
to cut these bars
and go outside.
But most to sing—
why not?
Is singing yet to be?
What was / is /
no, not by the waters
of a river,

James Joyce   or think a river runs.
I make no peace
a past.
If not to give delight
or pleasure
somewhere along its line,
then may it not be
death and dead
as these few moon stones?

What will you make of this?
more clarity?
I hoped for it,
and then gave up.
For:
          By the time
it cleared for me
the water muddied
far downstream
for such another man
as did not come here.
Listen to me:
(This is the cry all poets make.
So long as it is cry,
and not a moan,
I try to listen.)
What is it?
Out of singing, where a man
has broken faith

with fire and stone,
he may pick up reflection.
That is moon dust.
I do what I do
                in a hurry.
I am going out now
to try to shore up
something against a cold night
in the dead of winter—
waiting for its death.
and cull there:
                wood
                water.

Some have said
'superior'.
A being other than his ground.
And I will laugh at that—
go on.
Yes.
        Sing I must,
sing.
Can you hear the voice?
Is it a child playing—
or a 'bonded hero?'
But what's the difference?
Each sings,
is wise
in its own
way
goes down
to it
deeper than water
                depth
a threshold.

Or I counted lines again,
and took this out
of my belly—
tortured with an ache
that lost the liver—
knew I had no time
to think of that.

It bled and shrank.
But not Prometheus.
I had fire here
already.
Looked only for the fuel.
Took me in hand.
Take me out.
Not hard enough for love,
however you may take that.
Is it singing?
                oh - and -
always:
         Is it loss?

Book II

for Howard McCord

who knows why

XXXI

And for this part:
a part a pris:
Think:
Daily where I go from here.
HIS STORY,
make of it of such other times.
What would I do?
of what I did
what could I say?
I put it in the mouth
of horses—
                at a brazen place
I took it,
         and I linked it
with the past—
the future in it—
hoop snake with a tail
in its mouth.
We said no more,
              and then
we dropped it.
             We moved
away.
       Where we stood
we saw a place
closed off.
Well, that was the place,
and the past—
apprized.
We take it in from there.
At least -I do.
Whatever my part in it,
I remember one
who said, "At our age
we can no longer
speak of love
as actual. We are too old,
And we do not love
as we once did."
And I was shocked,

SS

not angry, but saddened.
What is there to speak of
outside of love?
Love which may at times
exclude an object—
(as its part)
but takes a context—
opens that one—fully.
It is there we take
a vantage.
Age has no bearing.
As if we were let in
to a conspiracy—
a place of misery,
something all men share.
"Welcome stranger."
I do not wish to go that way—
a path in a thicket—
thorns—
made easier
only because others are there.
A weakness—
throw and flux—
lit fires,
but lit to snuff out
in smoke and stink.

Now that I walk:
Halt—
and take to ground once more—
Metcalf Graveyard,   the first time out
Winthrop, Maine   to go to boneyards,
looking at one man's art
whose name I do not know
or care to—
what he made—
those loops and curls—
what the man had
in him.
Part?
    or part a pris?
Or what the man was?

Fictive - is -
the energy.
It was always right
that men knew art
as life—and knew nothing
of it as idea.
We are not artists
nor artisans
but men.
We have made
the complement   .
but we are not finished.
Part a pris,
and there it is—
was not—
the ravaged country
lying close enough.
Thin leaves on ground,
a locust grove.

And high wind
sweeping the early ground—
dry this year—
sticks and leaves—
spring air.
All night the sound of it,
stretching the wires
taut.
          I break
my strength in
fortune
               this
the dark March wind,
another winter
season of the heart.
Staked out
a future place
for it
          and
against it.
When all this comes
upon
crest at such place.

(Numbing
the chill
after the false
quickening—
a part a pris.)
        His story mentioned—
one makes a mention—
and a way in again.
Dense as the thicket
of the past,
I mean to go in,
go out again.
(how locked in place
the fumes ignite.

Augustus John of
Toulouse-Lautrec

And as the man said:
"Very serious work,"
when someone else
dismissed it:
"Dirty pictures."
I know. - I know.
A part a pris.

XXXII

Measure of words
Measure of the man
Not man who says them
Not cubit, foot, or li
put: 人木昌个禾条
How do you heighten it?
Dark growth on the north side
The deciduous ridge.
The diaeresis.
What cannot be contained
What is not singular
IT.
       And we have not reached

beyond it?
the touch.
                        The days of genius
are long days
                        stretching
star to star—
                        ideogram
to rune.
Measure of the sun
whatever span—
Elbow to outstretched finger—
distance—thumb end
to small finger.
                        Measure
as crystal to crystal.
                        Touch
tactile
          open dawn.

As a Druid or a child
might say it:
                "Take this branch in
and burn it now."
For purpose either?
Both will be cold, on winter night
both pray to life.
In howe or tomb—
ship's burial
                as
a burial at sea
slips down, leaves no sign,
unless, dark night,
the whirl of phosphorus,
oiled black surrounding it—
one measure of the man—
language and elision.
Hectare and acre—
rod, chain and link.
Does the land know its measure?
the man at its head pace out?
Towards the howe
                his coffin.

It reaches system,
                    touches death.
Measure cannot straighten:
Thumb to elbow.
Wind as familiar—the sound.   '
Requires it as courage—
signally
            goes on.

High barrow (cache)
bones
        arm bands
stone on sill—
shape
        the ship.
Prow to seaward—
out bent
            as land
caught on measure
takes it away
                    once more.
Complete
            arch and spine—
the high window—
pole of the ridge—
now it's season.
Herded or faced east.
(A certain distance
seen at all points.
Selved best.
Somewhere piled—
cairn and dam—
free stone—
association beyond leak
nothing more than marker,
grave—remembered.
A good man with stone.
Could you tell me
how is stone made?
No man may know.
No explanation,
                    and
no synthesis.

Give us stone.
mean and means that are good
with stone.
          Leave effigy
as one ideogram.

A mountain wind!
Blast of four days,
and at the coast
calm sea—
         the wind offshore.

That which knows nothing of me,
nor where I have been.
Like the buoy
        endlessly racing
nowhere.
        in flux of the tide,
downstream to the sea.
Cupped in my hands
a small part of it.
And of so many things
           these
memories:

Peggy Simson Curry   Of the woman
for whom the lake was named,
and what she said
of that old man
who did the naming.
Put it in his measure:
"Don't try to be more
than that grass.
It is enough."

And say no more
        of it.

Or that other:
"If two or more persons
go
in disguise upon the higheway—"
of such antique rhythm,
response,
        nowhere

flatfooted.
How can one release
or tighten in such places?
Should one?
Move straight on.
The sun: ☰
So to bathe in it.
I keep my hands in,
still cupped.
What the numbers are
or where they merge.
If I should want
to pull out stops or
stanchions, maybe I
would know *why* (?)
Usually I don't.
I touch such places
(bearing fire)
(conscientious)
now
            what does that mean?
We're all turning towards
some sort of realization.
Wouldn't you say
that the pine branch
this afternoon
meant something?
I'm not beyond it
                        yet.
How much of me
or you
            is undone?
Look!
            I want to walk again.
But if I do not,
as I fear,
                there are many places,
much that is rich,
                        still palatable—
open and with horizons (reach them.)
All in places opening and closing
on silent valves.

Make sure of them.

(I will.)

And I will live,
only because of measure.
What the measure is:
The sun.

XXXIII

If we remain too long
perfectionists
we believe in death—
pluperfect—and the dust
of fields laid open
in the fall
before dry winters.
We shall die and open
a frozen seed.

Complete?

Completion?

How in hell

to deal with that?
The pain is simple

pain—

and I am lonely,

in a crowd

which might be cloud.
Open up, and take from me
what I do not have to give.
Oh lord, and at what costs
what I might write off
the page

as well as on.

Good lord
you have given me so much,
and I'll walk
miles and mountains
once again:

againagainagain,
always my reverberation,
my sound,
       and echo
down the well.

Gustav Mahler #9   At this point listening
to gathering music,
large sounds
       and little bells,
dare not dispute me,
I have heard *those* sounds
long before
      gathered
for me.
       Touched on
good places.
As I heal
I'll rise up
into high air.
The mountain wind
         heard
a long way off,
      and
well,
    in other times.
Be close to me,
and love,
    not me,
but way of loving.
May,
    and may again.
Open,   opening,
fresh wound
or old one.
Let out the clots,
Lest they do not
dissolve
    away.
The old hard
      ship
dis
   ease

154

leaking itself
into the dark
                    ness
divided.
              Core of completion,
that which is perfect—
implies—

False bits and hopes
I cling to—
                    thinking
that any day improves
another
              or wipes out
its illness.
What is it that a man holds
hardest to?
or perhaps best
not to ask that question—
diffused and cracked,
as if the bones themselves
had split.
              How many?
and how often?
Names and days to
put it down—
                    a little further
to the west,
                    and men walk off
the edge of it,
no matter what was said,
or why the saying:
A little more than that
set down
              and by
whose fortune d?
By what precept
turn the edge?

Aroostook, April 1974   Well, this time removal worked,
and set me at it
once more.
Thriving on my own illness,
aghh!

155

why consider that?
a man moves
as he moves—
that is about all
once can say
                    of/for it.
Not looking for the smooth end,
take all of this—
splinters foremost.
Holed up—
away from men.
That's the best of it—
doing the work in blind surroundings,
nothing much to distract—
away from the street—
a short way,
watching the late snow settle.
Wondering why.
Well, they've all asked me,
and I've nearly answered.
It does seém good
to get out of my own doors—
to know there's damned little
else a man can have.

Cross such mountains
late in the year—
find such places unde snow,
forget the fragile take
of my own self.
Well, perhaps,
and to walk again.
The far north reaches
where a man's eyes water
constantly against the wind.
Teeth of the lodestar—
again
            we're at it.
All of such illness
takes its own shape,
and few are content
to remain inside and quiet.

E.P.

Something that asked me,
or prompted me to asking,
makes me the purist of myself.
That will forego
the other—
what is perfect.
I may admire at times
the look of one in earnest
who will not settle
for what is real,
and destroys it all.
But there are places
and patience.,
and these might be learned.
Easier to come by fortune
if it is taken
as it is,
not a priori***
as it 'should be.'
Never to beg the issue,
but to know it
for what it is.
Seize on
               and
hold to it.

Out of such small dreams
these things—
and the death of things
I had hoped to know.
In the story
there are events,
and I will not shift the blame
or
⎛ wonder
⎝ wander
SIMPLY
               that I will accept

XXI

things as they appear to be—
i.e.
    as they are.

Do not call in,
there are no answers left.
You made your own
as I had feared it.
I'll answer back:
A month of silence,
and a year of doubt:
In the month and year,
when all men try
and all have failed,
for such, their trying.

      XXXIV

Col
    Column
to which I tend,
am bound.
A cult in mystery.
Fixed in me.
Petulant man—His story—
equalled and equals.
Old men delete
and would revise.
They add:
        talking.
Age, not by snow
or calendar.
Will we listen to them?
Is that history?
Pass over.

I am asking questions,
not answering.
The phone hung up
with wires cut.
Keep them so.
A man works
at how and why he does.
The mechanics.
There are those who live by them.
Hard to crack that.
Take your teeth out
every night.
Convention and reality
what is of use,
which is which,
what is.
It is not only
what is pushed,
though pushing has
stress.
What is real to you?
How do you push that?
throw it in the teeth
Of those who take them out?
It is not a usual rebellion.
That is expected.
It is by doing
what is not known,
and cannot be censured.
All are capable—
few think so.
Becoming dark,
it is difficult to see,
but as a man
with the last things possible,
signing his name
as the light goes out,
a man must talk.
Age, but not because old.
Look for the place.
It is often pleasure.
I wanted to get the gist of it

through reading,
but not in reading words—
that is a way out,
and some things say it
clearly
with no sound,
no written character.
As no part of anything
except the space
that must sound—
that is—
(as objects are not.)
Once to speak it,
Once to take it,
live it—
no incision.
Never a rest.
Write it in:
in the work of a lifetime.
And if one does not,
in a life,
there is no rest - ever.
Or, as the man says,
it's in the works.
However it happens, bless you,
walk
by your own pace.
says it—fully.

Signet,
parsing of the text.
To deserve—
or what one needs—
place for beginning,
perhaps it will open
once more
into that col
roused up,
eventually box canyon—
the cul
Whatever it is
in mind one knows it

clearest—opening
outside of place—
the raveners
could have composed it
from little or many—
made on a cold morning
from dry tears.

Eddy Fontaine,
5/8/74

Those who come out:
'Well, er, when I was a boy
we all sat around
in the evenin'—
nothin' much to do, you know,
so we had axes and knives,
and we carved wood,
like we cut it all day.
I allus wanted to make fiddles—
no time until now.
I'm an old man,
but I like it fine.'
A way out of the cul
across col
to the column,
and not a raised stone.
This out of a day
when I was ready to hear it.
We hear nothing
until such time.

Dry tears,
or those imagined,
at the head of the draw
some salt
          dried
before it was sweat.
Take it back into
the body that needs it.
All of it may come from need—
a hard way to explain—
but there are times
when that stutter
and the erased tone
reverberate—

161

hit upon the place—
such place as a man
might find a way to food and water,
at least the usual.
A place to try it on
for whatever it might be worth.
(Measure not—
                worth is
whatever—
find it
        no coin
to change hands behind it,
or for it.
A day's wisdom
drawn from the work.
What else could a man take?
((Take?))
Well, try it.
No losses—
the others cut at sea.
Noting the stillness,
it is filled with sound
—beyond silence—
another affair.

It all comes to the place
where
that point of the story—
mine or his—
was or is—
may be—
all of it past—
stress these by a moment's vexing.
To cut or hold the strength
and hurt—
            the vehicle.
and the way—
column or col.

XXXV

The talisman as
          what is found
in the right place
the right time,
for one who understands or needs it.
That the centers converge—open,
that all is present
undiscovered until
the head
      turns.
Whatever is picked up.
One man, his eucalyptus pod,
to keep him through nights
of terror and sea wind.
Things found, and almost lost,
never surely—
one finds again,
out of anxiety the wisdom—
fear,
      and how a man
may quit fear by holding
in his hand,
slapping a pants pocket:
"Thank god it's still there!"
Salvage by moonlight.
There is no clear reason,
which is all of reason.
Hold on, the day comes,
with the talisman expended.
Halving the distance—
such as one perceives.

As in people:
At the moment when I had set
in motion
a danger—
the man answers
who blocks it
in his presence.
(No matter what the history,
Longinus' spear,

E.P.

163

a talisman for evil,
and not discounted.
Whatever the power,
it remains as we think it,
dies only in disbelief.
A man has done with seeing—
achieves vision.
Weight and substance,
light and heat.
Tensing a bit,
shakes himself and goes on.
(It is mistaken
to think of ending—
loss is not the end,
nor new findings.)
What shall I pick up?
Choice? Chosen?
both—
       and that other—
who shall find the found?

Homage to Keith Wilson

And it is the wind
far more than ice
            or water
flecks off the name
in stone,
or stone itself.
Whatever takes,
takes from the pleasure
or pain of one,
not touching those of another,
passes by,
but not in dimension.

Order of words—
What is order?
Words?
It is not arbited—
not seasonal.
Words break out—
order fails,
coheres as friction—
what may reach.

The wind picks up
and flails—
new leaves and blossoms
fall on bare ground.
Dust coheres to air.
No mixture.

Of timing,
          this coheres—
in the cohesive.
it is always a coming together.
'Synchronize.' Synchronize
and die.
It is not a timetable,
not a way to go from here to there,
fluid as mercury—
elusive as fish.
It is timing to be had,
and not to be held.
It is power.
It has its talismen.
One cannot do
          without it.
Most live that way:
no timestress,
snuffling the dust,
and spitting out the wind.
Try to make it,
not trying.
Sense his story.
(Or perhaps none at all.)
It is not paradox.
It is other:
on those planes
and those dimensions
open to us.
Few, but happy, go there.
Lyric of timing:
All men have said 'I',
meant it
          or not
as they were honest
with themselves or not.

Some learned a better word:
When.
And went out the door with that,
not in anger,
but sadness ith those
who say and say,
and say nothing.
Use of word
as the talisman
to give further.
Not heritage as bequest,
but for him who can take it
and leave it at the same time.
Is that possible?
Take your own,
and look beneath
for breath and stone and nails.
It gets said.
The words as inadequate
as they often are.
Take them into as much as you can.

George Oppen

Sometimes in poetry
a man speaks of poetry itself—
takes it as *his* talisman,
something he may hold to,
a bit of the dust of a world
larger than any galaxy.
What they sing,
and what they say,
never limiting who they are,
or holding merely to words.
That is timing, clarity, living.

As the man steps out,
the morning welcomes him.
He finds space.
There are no windows,
no faces pressed against them.
He is free,
            clear of it.
It will have changed by afternoon,
cold rain and fog

in from the sea.
Put up sail,
and search downwind for landmarks.
Whatever the talisman,
it is not luck,
whatever in the man
steadies keel—
keeps the sail out of irons.
He delegates less than he knows.
A broken distance,
line of rocks.
Perhaps he breaks through
above the mist.

A fiat for what one finds,
keeps or does not,
as the eucalyptus
after a long season
loses scent—
another dried shard.
Place a cup next the sun
to gather light,
and loses in a moment
moved away.
The burning glass forced
to a point
sets fire,
       races away.
As there are parables,
and are not.
A man taking his way
is always a man found out—
should be—
and he smiles and gives,
doesn't give a damn
for anything but his way,
wrenched or not.
Season or no season.
Holds whatever he has.
The talisman.
The grail is a goal,
and no answer.

Completes
            what ?
HA !

            XXXVI

Fragile
        light and heat
thin line against the sun
blots it out.
As red in spring
                is
red in fall—
            both fragile
to certain lights.
It is best in prose
to space it.
It is similar with light.
Against—
            more rarely—through,
as through creates a difference
or reflection.
                Heat slows it
cannot touch or keep
without direction.
Derived
force deflects,
lost somewhere outside,
and reasons merely
with a silence
beyond quiet.
It is a season
governed by the tilt.
Hard to forget it—
the fragile limit.
Taken out and into the forest—
rain, bending and swerving,
who cares for the sources ?

it is rain and wet.
To touch it—the moment—
how one may or may not.
Time of it—
beating against my cheeks—
walking again - free -
but free only of encumbrance.
It is not freedom.
The darkness of such woods—
the fragile light
held somewhere in suspension
above clouds—
more surely—above me.
Halfway down the page,
a place to set down
anything
(to avoid the source)
—and no one listens anymore.
The language is no large concern—
common as coin—
spot cash for understanding.
it completes itself
without the rain source,
or the word beginning—
there is no seed,
and there may *be* no more.
Impressed upon us—
lost - from us.

John Hodgkins

Or consider the face
of the young boy—
pale—almost delicate—
unhealthy.
He sits and broods
among the others.
Would like to speak out,
but doesn't dare—
pecking order of the shadows
around him.
Despair limits
where the light may be
and not be.

After Pittsfield The master came ten times. Each time he said but one word: 'Awareness.' He said it very softly, and his students kept on reading, dozing, or playing cards. They did not hear him. The master went away. He realized that he had taught them everything he knew. The students were already enlightened. The only light that is not fragile.

Heat, only in the cool
leaves, hanging
new and limp
in the pale fog
following a night's rain.
The way open finds
openings
among shadows—
thickets of them.
There are:
No / more / trees /

Jake at Stockton Sprs.

As the young boy says:
"Into those grey mountains."
A light less fragile.
Or how these violets
                              rehearse themselves
before they bloom.
                              What
it is for them
                    in frost
after a hot day.
How they survive,
and some of us do not.
Take it from whence?
W-H-E-nce-A??
Not a word,
the echoing from a prior well.
Always to be open
to that which comes in,
and remember who you *were*
                              at fifty,
from what you are.
Make that piece together.
How else could it be?
or who were you?
(I walk some of the same)
                              roads.

ROADS!
Take them. Make them.
not for your own.
As they are—
an escalation.

Exulting in this day
when all things are accomplished,
not a finish.
How they rise,
even in darkness
(there is little light.)
To make of them
more time
than might be had,
or one's own.
Time which is not counted,
not divided.
The way out there—
the way back in,
little is held,
or given.
Exulting in that day.
What do you do?
Where did you come from?
Are these the questions?
What before?
No, afterwards.
Nor did it end there,
where is the day?
Out of the annoyance,
the uncertaintly,
a feeling close to fragile—
what will shatter
almost as a storm of blossom—
what looses and loses
over a landscape,
shadow heat and light.
It has always been the light
that attracted me,
never the color,
although color may enter into it.

Light on the mountains,
some filtering late
into the valleys—
or when one is above the cloud—
fog below—
but there the clean light.
October is the time for it.
Whatever it is—
open or sealed,
two terms for the same.
How one rises in the morning,
or the evening—
                    at midnight
for a variation—
light and light—
and what light brings.
Wherever one can go
to take or find it.
I think it is time
to warm food—
eat out of the shadow.

XXXVII

Intuiting:
            What we read
                        or write
is not to be repeated.
Music—what one hears
fully—fills the body
with desire
            to come back
and back again.
                    Not back
to hear.
        To hold.
Seeds are like that.

No one tires of leaves
                    new
every / spring / year.
And for the rest of them—
how they quicken—
life as quick—
the only term into it.
Measure, and how the measure
of such music.
We are alive in it,
and the words—
                    these words—
speak sermons.
Unless they are sung.
Let us go to singing
for such pure joy
as may be found there,
or the profound sadness:
other singing.
Whence? Whence?
or only: to take the breath
to make the new phrase.

Gustav Mahler   As that young man,
circa 1880   breaking his song: HEIA!!
                       before the throb of the web.
Not only a young man—
an old man sings
his love songs,
if he sang before—alive to the world.
Mists that clear in early morning,
Dew given back to the sun.
The river is loud,
its spring voice rising
in light air.
                    Heia!
Whatever—
                    plain song or chant,
given back to the day,
music rises outside.
Comes in again.
Sound of the day,
sound of whom we are.

Thence. Thence.
Mention, and make note.
It was that clear tone,
and what was singing.

Mist of the dream appears and
disappears at the moment,
as the moment makes—
perhaps the man.
Does the man know?
What he would write down
vanishes
        like the pebble
over the cliff side—
roaring of wind on a dark night.
Did it reach?
           the bottom?
And the chance of being hooked
into the same places—
what was before or after.
Yét the music of the dream coheres—
and coexists.
The body is not free of it—
never can be free.
nor would it—groping
in a mist of dreams.

Or take this plant
set in the window—
left by a friend:
Patience, or impatience,
what you will to make it.
Glows—its one red flower—
is a part of dream,
or where dream rises.
Yet I see it,
        every morning,
fresh as sunrise—
flaring as the sun goes down.
All in all—
        might set up
a good day.

Mirage, which is reality—
gentleness complete.
Could take credence in it.
Walked out early
with no clothes, into the
temper of the air,
and after several days of rain
saw fields and trees
in dance again.
And so they do—
                    dance.
The staying on.
I do not take as permanence
any of these good cycles—
but believe in them
for what and where they are.
Knowing ends,
and what perception is,
what it implies:
A death of friendship.
As I know the man
to be a friend who tried
to buy me
with his kindness and his company.
Wondered what would end it.
(As I am not a friend
to sun or wind—
a fact of them.
He fears me now—
looking for that 'king's wind'
                                as
in the old poem.
I have such need and
wish for wind,

6/7/74   I cannot count it mind.
For those who do:
'Get the fuck out,
                    and stay out!'

Gustav Mahler: Still the pure music
Das Lied von der Erde from that night and day
#9, #10   Its passage.
How the distances are breached.

Where one goes for them.
Why go? or stay?
In love and out of love,
alive for all these days,
play on.
There is no end to it.
(Must at this point turn
to other affairs,
but it is not leavetaking.
It stays
           with.

Of all that heart, opened,
closed again—
motion which is music,
noise which is music,
simple sound
and simple silence—
what the music says:
In saying least—
or not at all.

John Cage

XXXVIII

Intensity—
           or white heat—
(red or blue or white.
So what about it?
Art doesn't improve
(nor do men)
They both change—not much.
So—what about it?
How does the change occur?
where?
           is it?
Do the seeds flower
to a final fire?
What is implicit?

Why should anything
                    be?
or have no being?
(Even in strong sunlight,
the threat of rain,
and the earth waits
                    swollen.
Breaking against it—
nothing but the head—
the darkness
                    assumes,
subsumes,
            a cloud—
Or smoke?
White heat, or workings.
A man goes out
                    What one finds:
The new words are old one,
the definitions flex and change.
There is no staying still.
If a man wants to
he is already dead,
buried under uneasiness,
and hardly able to move.
Making it on any way
is a process unlearned.
There are no secrets,
no masters and no failures.
It is always the moment
of / in / tensity—
where rightly his stay
comes alive again.
Whatever it is—
pay heed only to the tightening
inside—
everything else loosens,
soaks off the label.
(Put out your head
for whatever beating.
It is easier in the long race.
Few who will acknowledge,
but we do, as a whole,

get it in the neck.
Intensity
            to go with clarity.
As, when a man hears
of another's death—
those forces still at work.
But realizes that there is nothing
further to say.
The man said it all for himself:
"we carry our own crises within our heads."
Death may not be the last,
but is the last we know.
Whatever we build from that,
let it be intuited /
                    / intense.

And on grey mornings,
light just such a fire
as takes the chill
away from edge—
but leaves the cold insdie
to work its own fires.
Giving by reason of—
that will not be said—
or touched
            easily.
Wherever a man may set
what strength he has,
climb up with ardors held
across the shoulders—
within the gut.
(or what a man may feel
in that recess
which remains a proper mystery—
that he does not know
what 'ails' him,
or whence his health—
his own state of it.
The ardors!
Let the ardors bloom!
The strong scent of them,
of sweat and musk,
enough to put across

Stuart Z. Perkoff,
6/25/74

178

or carry through—
let the shoulders bear—
but not all the weight,
and what is half-said—
generalized—
but concerned with the particular.
No talk of scythes,
or age as a condition—
remain open.
vehement for a just death
as a life,
        not of convenience,
but of a strength
beyond commonness,
reviving the most common.
It *must* be held
        inside.
call for the gut—
coil its spring for action.
The stroke
within limits
        the boundaries
being the strength.
The intensity disperses
without hold or chain.
It is the anchor of itself—
recognizing, in its fury against it :
No. All things, nor men,
not equal.
There is no equal try.
The lie of the ages
that it should be thought so.

Nor, with the difficult plan—
perhaps a letter
I do not wish to write.
Beginning towards another day,
and counting on few of them.
It is by such time
or such length realized
that strength comes
limitless—
denying the end—

divisible, but by other means.
Many hands in that,
and many cries,
many crises.
Time was not ripe—
the spaces between it.

Men who hide much of themselves,
in whom the animus is split,
whose good shows through evil—
evil *more* evil,
and little good.
It would be well if they showed us
the unlovely first—
that we might not trust them,
or feel that numbing blow
which is the death of friendship.
Or the animus when split
twists like a snake,
breaks out of them,
leaving a dry husk,
something hung up,
an ear of bygone corn
in an abandoned loft.
Such do not bear their crises,
do not die well.
Often, feeding on the young,
they destroy and corrupt,
when there is nothing left
in themselves to infect.
For them, intensity is reflection,
hollow, heatless light—
not with the moon's mystery
or silver—
but lead scrapings
at the bottom of a barrel of bones.
They shake loose in every wind,
howling for alms
which they do not deserve.
I have known such—
all of us have.
They are enough to poison us
against intensity,

against love of man for man.
Somehow we must guard against them.

There are others
rooted in integrity,
meaning the one:
                the integer,
who make up for it.
Seek them out.
They will replenish the world.
The single man,
lavish, and given back,
even in what they take and consume. .
So the late adventures
open themselves to me.
This is what they have told me,
in that both are known to me.
Their stories—
and their flesh—
makes it possible to go on,
sorting out the kinds of heat.

Each fire one lights
a different fire—
flame and weight and heat—
ingots or peat—
blaze or glare against
how much smoke?
Where to begin it?
Blow on which coal?
One winks out—
or snuffs into dampness,
relapses—
another melts the stone around it.
as on the day the rock broke
after the sun had passed.
It is a tenuous time—
assaying it.
            Intensity:
What is high or low fire.
A time to leave it—
to put the meld,
               alembic,

into the crucible.
Nether or upper.
Fire which gives
so much as charred ash
with bone or coal,
fern or maple—
lava flow spreading,
cooling—the form intense
under snow.
It will all pass its own way,
leaving nothing
                but the change
which is heat—
which is not weighed or measured
(the blinding flash.)
Open to it—
those who walk abroad.
and that time comes
as it goes,
never felt until past.
A fossil
        underfoot.

XXXIX

I have never seen you naked—
which I would say to anyone—
not knowing them enough—something
to know more.
It is not merely an interest
in young girls with nubile breasts.
I am susceptible.
Socrates—any old man whom I love,
for whom I have respect—
without the clothes?
                        yes?
Any clothes.
            (Not to pander,

or settle as voyeur.
I *want you* naked.
What will I know of your story?
if I see only from the neck,
and the cuffs
                    down or up?
If you can vaunt it all out
in another way,
I'll not ask you.
Most of you can't.
Places where you'll give me a hard-on,
I hope so!!
If I like you enough to ask,
that should enter.
What is this hiding?
You must have *something* to hide,
Not what you tease with,
as something better.
I have never seen you naked,
and I want to.
                    As the tree—
never before *that* tree:
Linden, linden, kiss the sun.
Where, and wherefrom.
Linden, linden,
                    kiss—.

(And I would think you might
reach home
                    before another shower.
Success to you.
I like walking there in such weather—
damp, pitch, and coming darkness—
the smell of the way.

Stream swollen—
where the tree stood—
a gap
        broken fang,
it is hard at flood
to guess the place.
A few landmarks to go on.

Still the call—
grace of a young girl:
Linden, linden, kiss the sun.
You do not hide your nakedness—
Linden, linden
                    kiss—

Reading it
            aright—
place after place is closed,
and there are no openings
wedged in thickets—
of the mind as well.
Makes for an interlude—
carries on through—
humor to go with grace,
dark wrestling angels
pause,
wipe sweat from their eyes,
grin, and go on.
Testing the rough places,
that they are still rough—
somehow more bearable,
and
            despite the clothes,
I may see through to nakedness.
What is not easily
or uneasily given,
becomes suddenly available.
Blind rush of it—
what is done
on an early morning.
Cutting the staff to fit—
as it touches the hand,
to not cripple or wither
the hand itself.
Find, among the flowers,
one that is not the same
in color, weight, size or scent—
differs.
            Not that it surpasses,
except in difference.

Is not less.
Find it, and you will have found the key,
lever,
                    capstone,
source of all of us—
for it is *us*,
                         not it.
Then take it,
                         in the eye,
in the ear.
In all senses.
At the same time, leave it
where it is,
                    to grow.
Know that it is fact,
that it is legend—
that blood is in it
as blood and water
                              shed.
Other blood must leave
and die.
                    Find it
first.
Simple enough to begin with.
It thrives in any garden,
does not demand a special soil,
withers only by greed,
or lack of recognition.

Iris, the clear eyed,
how the eye clears—
where it clears,
holds the blood of a glance—
thin—
          the wild one
from the bog.
Then what makes a sense for it?
not be revealed
until the day itself.
Moment—more than enough—
few find it—
fewer hold.

As the dream
and body cohere—
the time where they may.
But the iris and the linden
                              fade—

even
        fall.
It becomes clear,
The quiet supervenes.
Mention is open to us,
but rarely stance,
once the stance is taken.
It is time to go,
not to break.
Not to leave.
                    Simple enough to begin with.
It thrives in any garden.

XL

Side-tracked,
                always,
from the old stories
to his story of the moment,
which is more surely
the mainstream.
(Put it all in a dark binding,
and never know the difference.

This is the ony way
                    I can talk about it :
Dear Pam,
            Send me some poems,
not what you have just learned
or heard,
            and not to finish,
or finish with.
                Cut off its head
if need be,

I won't quarrel with that,
but,
send me something—
                    not what you spit up
undigested as:
                unfelt.
So I would say of this—
                    the lyric
becoming formula.
How can I listen, or dare listen?
Whistling in the dark again,
what's out of its dark binding
Listening now, to the few small drops—
a new rain—
            an old one,
and it is not finished,
will not set itself
as whole between—
a part—
        as I am.
Wind and drought—
no thought of it
                one year
-not now—
            the dust
assails.
Who will ask that?
as if it were question?
Turn the key—
dark hand—
make no mention more—
or let it be
the sidetrack.
One track leading from another.
Close or far,
barely made it inside
on that one.
The shower close as missile.
I am inside/
            /it.
Come to think of it,
but not to come that way.

The yeast rises
in its old manner,
coheres as it swells apart,
the many clusters,
many openings,
asssays,
       no more.
Dear Pam, let a man think
a bit,
     but not too much.
Kept asking for the way
to be -
      it is /
         / not.
Climbed over the storm—
the jewel weed—
reed of playing
in the wet.
As it *be*.
It is—
and climbed in again.

Track made in grass,
meshed as mashed
against the wet ground
below it—
the rocks. I had
hardly thought it there.
I went on— climbing.
Came in on the rope
of the morning—
the light haze
that burns before it clears.
I mind so little
in so many words.
They asked me out,
neve fear that,
having known the dream.
Old axles broken
           on the
side / track—
used too little—
positioned on light ballast.

Came in here,
went—
        the light is fading.

The other man,
who spent his mornings fishing,
to get away from any track.
Knew only one stream,
counted it
        not main nor side.
Feast of reprisals
        in the sun
too hot to bear,
or to bear with a different day.
Coming down out of the woods:
"Here's your breakfast,"
And the fish,
        rotten with heat.
Not planned, a sadness.
Anger which is not angry,
out of the sun.
The way the man asked
gave no quarter or pardon.
Listening to it:
Is it only in that place
that the body and dream cohere?
Have basis in the world
we know and handle?
Do you know
what it is to ask these questions?
whence a man goes out of them?
Why he goes?
Who or what
        is / does
he?

Mentioning the row of trees,
or the row of notes / sounds,
what is between them.
How many places for the sidetrack?
or can it be called such?
properly?
We've worked our way through,

have found little past
or before.
Yet it is the place
where hub and tire
belong to the wheel
long past.
I'll climb there one morning,
where the rain falls
on rock.
Few plash ponds.
Marshes below.
Dry heather country,
and the taste of ashes
older than the world.

Haydn

Setting the best clothes on,
or aside.
It makes little difference.
Spending strength on
                        climbing up.
There are those who would rather look
from below.
I cannot quarrel.
They have a place in it.
The mass and the weight,
hip and shoulder,
are more than the top,
except for the clear air
beyond.
Climbing into that
without its limits.
Composed of such difficulties,
thrust by the yeast,
but in coherence
the tracks and the sidetracks,
the sidings,
where one waits.
To assail distance—
to live closely:
A handful of precepts,
a quiver of arrows.
A man takes over
what takes him over.

There is no difference.
Dear Pam,
              again the letter.
I do not know
what to put there.

XLI

Anger of a door
                slamming in
on itself—
                on summer breeze
-northwest-
                that took the rain away.
brought edge,
                hammer blow
that shifted weight, and
slammed the door.
It was not:
                Anger in myself,
the door,
              the wind,
that surcharged anger
-electricity-
                a thunder.
What the world brings home to itself,
an impartial assay,
without morality,
                or my thinking.
Just so we look at
                all things,
men. and distinct from men.
The door
              slams /
shut.

How you would weigh
                pass / impasse,
not as a man's flesh,

or a part of what
                    and how
you weigh.
Face, in the work,
                    who you are, and
you fact it.
                    Nowhere else.
The work flies off from you,
not where.
There is no question—
no need to take a book along
for singing.
How many times I've said this,
but how much
                    each time,
it needs the saying
                    more.
Facing—always the facing/
/ saying
          thins away—
the sound constant—
at / a / distance.

And on a hot day
(midsummer,
                    which I often mistook,
pronounced 'mead'—
                    a drink for summer)
the teacher bird above the stream—
something more to listen to.
Ask him what he teaches.
He laughs it:
                    'Teacher, teachah, teach'—'
That is all there is to say,
or what he knows—
                    (overtly,
the door slams.
Whatever one thinks of it,
there is little in thinking
that can lend to that fixed act—
clarity—
where the sun shines
clearer than in air—

no final place.
Nothing between.

I have thought at times
that I would live long,
that there was merit in it:
Virtu
     sisu,
perhaps 'αριστῆ
I am no longer sure—
nor sure that I should be there,
if it is.

Jonathan Williams   The man writes
'VIVAMUS'
         and I like
the exuberance - am unsure
that it is a place for me.
Near enough,
to have come thus far.
Take care, and move over.
Do I know,
       or did I ever,
' the sound of mountains '
as I thought of them.
We live, not until we die,
but until we no longer live.
Is that an ethic?
        An edict?
Did I have the right to say it?
or did the door slam?
perhaps catching someone's fingers.
Anger, but impersonal anger.
Anger—as if the red star
burning through the trees—
late at night—
fading slightly in the coming
sunrise—
      caught it.
Swallowed in land mist,
the breeze dies.

As the child says of it:
"The harp is like a brook.

The sound is falling water."
Or the harp takes off from there.
A literal stance,
                        as things *are*
where they are.
But with imagination.
Few combine them.
The breeze dies.
The breeze dies.
The door slammed—long ago—
and the literal
                        becomes
litoral—
margins of a sea—
Of air.
            the uncharted
calling across.

The implicit variables—
constant and consistent.
What if they were not?
Change as arbiter, or
none at all.
Clothes fit the man
or season
                whatever
implied.
The morning whipped with fog—
shreds of it hanging on near hills.
Down   out
                    or into it.
Moving by strength of it.
Variation.
                Implicit chance.
A light shood out—
matched in silence.

(Do I owe you a letter?
I no longer remember
                            easily
such things as:
                    I will/
will not/

194

as will be done.
I say I will to myself—
so will it.,
                    Do I owe you—?
So—on a rainy night—
to sit inside
and listen
            sometimes
dropping everything else
to hear it—
a good night for that.
Listening, listening.
If the door were to slam again—
its anger muffled in the wet.
The wind has all of it—
ghosts—
and we are close to the sea—
if not the place,
the feel of it.
The water flowing down again.
Drought ended,
if there was more
than slightest hint of it.
Perhaps?
            Nothing.
The sigh of the earth—
replenished
            and replenishing.
Listening.
It is that music
taken from the 'tune'
and used—
all substance drained from it.
Wrenched and
                    wrung out.
A place to listen—
a complex structure.
Rain again.
            And I revive
like any flagging leaf.
Come to it—
as if the bitter hadn't been.

The wind blows—
                    damp enough.
Plangent.
                    Water on the roof.

(That cleared.
How much is spent?
What was lost?
Tough rind and hide—
to bear the sun.
Believe it open.

Only that sound, insistent

Beethoven: Opus 106   that I listen
that I take to it
myself.
That place.
Who heard it?
Lonely   thin   air.
A taking off—
                    the mind,
or the limit of the mind,
gone beyond.
Never to come back.
A placement.

The door slams
                    again—
no anger.
                    Resigned,
not given up.

XLII

Symphonic Movement

TRIAD

(sections XLIII ★ XLV)

XLIII

Curious.
    Say it as many—
meanings or bearings.
Antiphon and telling
      of
openness—
    the death
which opening
      expands
it
  close as closed.
Let it—
    quietly
all out
    through
all through
     through
out.
(Or the leg swollen to the knee
impedes it
     in undress—
floundering.
     The night goes away,
grey light and
more light.
The bearings become
      moorings—

reflection below tide—
the antiphon.
Running from one to another—
points touched—
                    left.
Moths above cabbage—
restless.
            Going on.

Of nights, say,
in which the shape changes:
A black frog,
the voice of someone known—
once loved.
                Is it all reproach?
or does it come,
a voice from silence,
as the sound of silence,
as that sound of terror,
dumb
        numb
frozen?
The coffin nailed,
                        and earth not dug?
some kind of burial
with a sense of life still on.

Look you!
I walked today,
where I have not walked before,
having walked the route often.
A place—but not a place.
And could I find good browse?
place for a deer's nose?
A sight, say?
or how it works outside,
back through the place
where I once walked.
To take only so much,
                        as curious—
one is.

She said of stars,
'I try to know things,

P.S.M.

                              but,
too old to learn well.
Only a little browsing.'
Tell it as it is.
                    His story.

Chameleon—
                    quicksilver.
moving—and silent.
Ghost time—
and no place to rest,
as how the time falls due,
ghost time—
                    or free.
Mention, lack of it,
delight in things,
                    whole things,
seen from far off,
details or blurs,
smear of color,
all of this
          delight.
Could time stop there!
A portion of it—
browse through:
a rumination.

Or as the line in a dream:
"Because there is no hill"
Where would that have been?
Why does it come here now?
Among these much loved things—
A circumstance unknown
since that late night—
and flaring Cassiopeia.
All that becoming story,
out of past,
               to past—
this future.
Whatever any of it—
means
          or meaning.
To the catch—

                    pry and lever.
Whatever the place—
the meaning of?
Take the time to touch it.
Glass clouded from a breath—
opening - closing.
Make of it as much
as may be.
Senses awake—
fur erect—
intensity passed by—
slipping to another.
As of such times,
the fever grows.
coming in and going out.
These fortunes
                    told in series—
curious,
          as I sleep.
And as I wake,
                    the curia.'
Equals care.

          XLIV

To observe:
                    Everything.
To hold all things in tow
(or sway)
to make of them
what is made,
                    or more.
To walk a way
which is 'aways'
but to hold on each thing—
the rapt face of the listener.
But—
Does it happen that way?

Sets for itself some specious stage.
Can it be, always,
that it is at this point?
Or does the attention,
                          in
and out,
            serve more?
How do I arrive at his
                          (my)
story?
Spending the days at it,
I abjure,
            or walk out
in the middle of the harvest.
(The only way
to get it all in.
Made and making—
not the only-
                    a— —.
Way is a way—
                    "aways"
away.
            A weigh.

Or to observe too much—
the head
            tilted
at angles on angles—
grows weary,
cannot contain—
                          neat categories
opened and closed—
boxes and jaws.
All are open,
and too much closes.
We'll leave it at that.
Or the man straining,
"what was that?
Why didn't I hear it?"
Heard enough.

10/5/74   And the face of the mountain—
once more—

with the old friends.
A voice from another past added.
It becomes right agan.
'Careful for nothing.'
Note it.
In all these places of tenderness,
wherever that might come from,
I see and hear what it is
that prompts me to say it,
and yet I have gone nowhere
into it—
                    flitting and veering
Moody Beach   until eventually I reach the ocean,
rest for a moment on wet sand.
Weight of it against my wings
until I die in the tide.
Literally, what I have seen there,
only yesterday.
                         I cannot reach
Surinam withthe others,
but that is a place of slaves,
and I will do well to stay on—
without harm
                    the possibilities.
The turn is direct—
                         becomes
again the fate :
"Careful for nothing."

Moving,
          and the roar of the sea all night,
fades into morning sounds.
The ground mist rises.
A late warm day—
Indian summer.
Moving on again,
                    among voices—
the last colors.

All that a man may know.
So little of it counts
for more than he counts it—
except as he counts.

As if he said,
"Jeez, I move five hundred cubic yards
of stone."
(or read so many pages.)
"He speaks sixteen languages."
"Climbed Mount Everest."
To what purpose?
To experience everything—
nothing but the flux—
as the tide returns
to where the tide has been.
A man makes much of it—
or does not.
Two dates on a tombstone—
maybe none—
                no stone at all.
Can't speak,
            and can't say
on
    what one says.
Examinations in pure hatred.
Note these days carefully.
To observe is
                over the ledges
counted carefully—
nothing left to count.
Auction it all off—
sold for an empty shell.
Made certain there is—
no one knows it.

At such a point
                being
the sound of the leaves
or
    in cloudy weather
could it be rain?
Poplars late in the year—
here/
    /high
at the new place for working.
Earlier, the small nugget—
apples held like a fist

—three of them—
at the end of a branch—
no others.
Tree weighted down
                              merely
by weights of the year.

Say it!
              Say it clearly.
The doubts are yours, old man,
as you grow old,
                              older than you like,
passing in and out
over the pavements—
where there's a new chance.
That will say little,
but this afternoon, on a late swim,
do not forget
to bring back the flat stone
as a doorstep.
Think forever to make
forever
              as the only disaster—
turns bloodstains—
places them

Hawthorne / Bucksport   on

gravestone
or doorstep.
Whatever a man hears—
he hears it most
                              as complete
in his own
              door / yard.

Do not take notes,
or if you do,
let them be incomplete—
fragments—
the only way one finds
the listing
              of it—
whatever it is.
Dutiful following of the thread—

weights and
        maps of it.
Precarious impingement.
And I will listen
for a little while
to all that sound outside—
the poplar trees
late in the year.
Heard and over
        heard—
as if, yes,
        the pun for it—
heard.
Take me out once more
to find—
well—
what is it that a man finds
if he rehearses
ghosts ?
that tablature ?
Can a man come in on that ?
I have never been able to say
so much.
Bending now,
over a new table,
touching the clean edge of it.
Fire too warm,
but early morning
        such
a fire is there.
Could it be anything else—
sane
    (as sane must be)
Dutiful following of the thread
weights
       and snaps it.

XLV

And what did I think, this day,
to take?
        put solely in the rain
to melt or wilt?
The snow - to freeze?
Or did I
        all these things at once?
Need I ask?
I have the place, and the stance—
(the three) ((that one between))
pre-history—
pre— story of what I know—
or dò not.
The where, and how to so begin it.
It is, if it applies at all,
a flash,
        galvanic,
touching
        perhaps that land:
"Vestri Obygd,"
never known,
always known.
Why do we look?
forward or froward—
to take the breath away.
Know everything in an instant.
One, or such another one.
Break the shorings or moorings—
whatever is needed—
             to take off.
Some do—
        and some will not.

Time for the time of it
            to
flow
   down
taken
   and glazed in
the last window—

as a window faces
                    out,
not south as I think,
                    nor east—
simply out again.
Could be,
            a window
seen :

What do they do ?
                                behind those windows ?
opening
        on a wall ?
Two foot facade
above the store below,
fleshing it out,
or not at all.
If there is window tax,
let the assessors know this one.
Somehow an outrage
on a cold night.
Time
        for the time of
                        it
to
    flow
        down.
Triad :
To reach omniscience,
no saving grace—
no reason for the man
so
    caught.
Galled in his own
heart strings.
Hurry with a broken neck
until dead—
yet—would not have it
another way.
Trial of this way,
error,
and the sweetness—
death with no sound.

207

Might we all
go this way
(and no subjunctive.)
Tensed for terror—
who will hold the line?
Who, in his fact,
has ever known it?
Reported in his story—
Taken as a part,
but then the whole,
might be omniscience.
I know that much of it—
at any rate had it clear—
thought by this
to reach another day—
turn another page
before this one shrivelled.
Something drives on—
the little sound
of penmanship.
Turning in :
Then :
        Must do good.
Iterate
        (or re)
Time for
        the time of it to
flow
down.
Trying—as ends meet—
to reach the beginning.
What did I take this day?
or was this day
that one?
Such a distance—
I'd hardly found it—
only now,
as the spilling leaves
might have stripped the poplars.
(And I *know* that
at this distance.

No problem :
                    gnosis.
Can be the joy of it—
and from.
Take in the sheets
redeemed.
Will get back
to that other
in another voice—
set of them
                    as
chest of viols—
families of such instruments.

Rhyme—
one and the same
                    with reason
seems to be—
                    old sense—
that one of rhyme.
A squeaking whistle of the marker
on a page—
some reason—
                    rhymed
into sense of it—
but follow—do not
attempt to build it up,
or set it there.
Remeber me in glad tide
coming over
                    as the rhyme
will not.
Attempt the strength of music—
clear as water—
this, untrembling
                    in the socket of a well—
last drops distillate.
Or once
put forward.
How the man sings out—
the shell of him.
Lying in the unknown house
with such a woman—

she unknown—
never to come back to it.
Lease or loose,
on time,
             bare heaven for it.
(Time,
        for the time
of it to
        flow down.)

And lying in that bed
at night
             above the chicken coops.
(Daly City, many years ago)
I dreamt of stones,
                 of one bored through
by water.
            Amulet.
Found it, beneath the bed,
at morning.

Spent it all—
                an area reclaimed,
spent or found—
few differences.
Take what you know for
what you don't,
                and call it
square.
Out of all these places
to something sure—
a man walks on,
head bared,
hands deep in his pockets,
(habit, and not thought)
that he may be seen,
or not seen.
It is the bright corner.
Walking out,
                may not come in again.
Time,
        for the time of it,
to flow down.

What may be done here?
What shards break first?
Kicking among old leaves and bones,
what do we see?
Who is there?
behind the smoke?
we have met few men,
left some of them.
The road that disappeared
behind that mountain
takes most of them
to easier country.
What do we hear?
Whom do we know?
Not for all of it,
put time within
and
      go   along.

XLVI

It is not unusual
to talk what is strange,
to be a long way
from the average whinny.
But is there any/thing to say
about that?
         except
that a man lives where he is?
damned well better know it?
Why do these bell wethers,
whining members of the herd,
put on a loving smile of guilt—
prize the outsiders?
It isnot pure envy,
although some of it
comes through as such.
It is the impotence of people.

Take them from where they are / not.
We'll get along.
It is not usual to live
away,
(it is popular,
                        few or some
do it.
Why have I come this road?
Somehow it fits, as a glove,
or the axe fits
                        in a hand
gloved or not.
It is a good place—
the place of the gut
—aching at times—
things you do not say,
knowing your own indulgences.
But to be a man
                        is to elude
the others.
Put that in your notebook.
It is
      what
it is not.
Let that be the lesson.
Learning is not the law—
let it flow out.
Have it separate.
Yes—to know
the usual as it lies.
What will you tell me?
Very little I need to know.
I put it all on paper,
and leave
for inside country.
Again the sections
of agony,
            wide sky,
and I will be enclosed.

Take up, and put up,
bell wethers—wethering.

As we have this-
                    of
"on the hook",
what will I believe that
                    to be?
What is?
I pick up from another's
fire,
but I am burning my own fuel,
no matter who lit the match.
Don't forget that.
We don't *all* think so.
We think as we know,
and that is dissimilar.
Well, most like to think
of a common fire.
I cannot—and do not—
my passion counts elsewhere.
All of yours does.
Get out—guys—
you guys—
there is a story,
yours and no one else's.
You don't want that?
Get off my life.
I have this place.
High up,
            even altitude counts,
and I will not break it
or sell it,
            or give it.
Put another stick in the fire.
I talk of it, because I do it,
not a concession to anyone.
Take a vacation?
Hard work, that.
Most are not up to it.
Writing fast, now,
always the signature
put on the page—
no way to avoid it,
might take it off later,

if it would rub out,
some corrosive
                    burn the eye of it,
possibly not, and hard to try.
One time wrote something:
'Well met—'
could not do it now.
The time of fortune changes
more than place.
A hold behind my door,
and if you come here—
fall in,
It is not the brute resistance,
neither do I resign.
Come forward on a little day,
By the fluke
flake
      flick
of the wrist—
                    a thing. king:
It is not your cities
that will ever make it,
                          not
your argument,
                    or my anger.
Daily,
      I see your sills
                    rot.
And there
         (even there)
                    what refuses to die.
Men!
      (I will talk to men,
not out of hatred.
                    Men,
you are wrong—
have always been wrong.
Your systems never challenged
a spider's web—
nor the spread of a raccoon's foot.
Should I ask you?
What can you tell me?

Men?
That vacant space
where a decayed stump stood.
Men?
Where the men?
Who are the men?
I tense,
          within,
about them.
Perhaps I had better stop.
Men.
Who / where /
are the men?
What it keeps saying:
Who are the men?

XLVII

Entered,
          solely
as the shape of old mountains,
taken as so many whalebacks.
Think of the places
                    named so.
And I, too,
          see them
spume
          spout
over weathered horizons—
on tall sides
                of the day
wherever
              sun—
sol—
          may be.
Or for comfort
                solace
as

       alone
solitary
        lit in to the bone—
whatever stride
                might have
hit—
        entered
in
    toward
level of day
            transit—
the back of the stove.
Bone mountain
                appeared
and appearing
apart.
        Interred.
Interdict.

Playing with such strangled keys,
or looking as I might look
It was a day for singing.
All that I can say of the day.
While such a day
                made of the mountains
more than mass—
                their shape and wieght
a tone in color.
Went there slowly
            as by eye,
stepped on the air
a long way back.
Well, we had heard this—
trying all we knew,
then struggled forward.
It was not to reach,
but to know the reach—
the grasp
        of it.

(We make more of it
than there is.
It all eludes us.

Keeps its shape:
                    the whaleback.
Flattens
          moves on
west—
          country of miasma
and then lakes,
                    remembers
the whaleback.

Aorta:
          as I said once,
high.
          It is heaved there.
Blood over the whaleback,
the glistening hulks ashore—
chased from an unfriendly sea,
or the land, flat pool

mid-Nebraska
11/74

groaning in pestilence,
imposed rape
                    supine
without pulse.
Hay stacked as monument
so long it blackens
and gives root.
Small windmills turning
without pump.
The whaleback nowhere in sight.
And night for scansion.
It ends.
          We resume.
The sharper spine of the earth—
still fluxing,
flow of the light and the sky

Wyoming, 11/74

together.
Take heart.
A different breed of whale.
His story,
impersonal as earth.

The shape of new mountains,
Plumes of their clouds,
men drifted away.

Smoke / spume / snow.
Could there be enough?

Thinking again of the whaleback—
the light fades slowly.
Shading the eye.
                Form emerges.
Tune of the wind,
there are no ages,
no categories,
history dissipated—
               not

Arminto, Wyoming   his story.
Dense completion?
ground to the sills,
the weathered outcrop.
Taking a turn in the clouds
for very wind that died.
His story.
Such as see—
to find it.
Lift
      ing

Wind River   the feather bones
  Reservation   antelope,
             deer
young colt or coyote,
whatever it might be—
insistent that it is not—
the last red burst of the day
against sand
            stone
as red,
      dulling
against the sky.
Chill comes—
too sharp for the whaleback.

Thinking of clouds
            as I did,
I stayed close to the land,
picking among patches of ice,
sugaring of snow

218

on the high ranges.
Why?
        Why is life hard
when these things open
to it?
A tense forming—
the groundwork
               placed.

Wind River Mountains   I climbed over ruins,
11/20/74   old bones in salt creeks,
smell of thin air,
sage,
and pure darkness—
almost light—
is it possible?
Is it made so?
thinking at random,
what makes light flicker
in such places.
(An assay:
Beam and the routed.)
And at random,
these voices:
The heart of the knowing
                      is
in these high shadows—
once early—
             once
late.

In high country
no theories:
This ice.
That snow.

Climbing on
             the top of it
recedes
        flattens
and rises,
        or the skin
of the earth flexes

over again
            tense—
in that past
            slow change.
The rise of familiar ground:
The whaleback.

XLVIII

Thinking of it—
            carefully—
if at midpoint
            I may see both
where I have been,
            and where I am going,
how is it I do not see back
from either end?
            Simplistic,
it may be explained in cases,
or in that last of senses:
            what is common.
As vulgate.
            Yet, I think of this,
and cannot find my way across it.
Who can sustain such flights?
Where would I take myself,
if the bow were bent
another way?
Look you.
I am standing in the snow,
near that fine old apple tree
that scants its fruit late years.
I look back to the outline of the house,
its angles, ells, and smokes.
I look up to the hill ahead,
see that place to which I am going,
to think, or work,
            or both.

Beyond the tree,
                I lose the house.
It puzzles me,
            as it does
in transit
to go from one place to another,
lose or gain in time,
dependent on the sun
and where the sun is left
or overtaken.
I will not settle for easy explanation.
Cannot sleep that well at night
for want of knowing.

It is a brave thing to set out
in the known world—
commonplace in that we do not know.
There have been times,
but I will not speak of them.
It is not enough,
and seldom wise.

(Where this mere paper
has been with me
before receiving what I write
is more than story—
given over—
            given up.

Yet I keep on
going
      sounding
wherever - what
the surprise.
It builds along such lines.
We all may know this
one day—
certain—
          as the next one falters.
Thinking out loud—
I merely reached for there.
It began to happen
once more.

Some new residuum—
some place that words flow
or strike,
or bounce, or miss—
heading into the—
                    ha!
abyss is easy,
like the explanation of places
seen midway.

Spice, and spice islands,
anywhere.
There are no long voyages,
though the way
seems long.
Comes in all of a sudden,
I like the French for sound:
tout a coup.
My eyes have seen
what your eyes haven't—
and yours have done as well.
But then this problem—
distance—
                    the middle distance—
keeps arriving.
When may I?
When do I salvage stasis
out of travel,
                    or
travail?
I think of those who do not move,
myself as
                    physical
rebels at this.
I must know.
Climb or swim,
know what it is there—
follow these backwoods and pastures.
But these others are right,
                    too.

There is that terror,
travelling where there is no movement,

and one stays
put.
All the tools sharpened,
but none of them to use,
or see in use.
It is a hard business,
going on.
Some have welcomed me,
fear, perhaps,
who would keep me on.
I do not see this world
as many do.
Sorrowing, I turn out
when the rain and wind
are hardest on the face—
the back of the neck.
Now,
          where is that?
Somehow I lose the thread
at moments when the skein
is most in hand,
but do not.
I am living!
Reaching out to
whatever it was I wanted
long before I knew
to reach.
(Others grabbed off the goodies.)
I think not.
I'll travel on.
This way—a mercy being
in this way.
I touch,
          and leave,
and touch again,
as back is back
or at the place
where old Ben Davis' tree
allows one right
to both.
No camp.
          No stop.

Thinking of it carefully.
How does a man
think? take care?
Some of us raise hackles,
soon subside
as cold numbs.
Thinking that we will change
what will not change
by our sights—
small place that a man may be.
(Taking over the land,
carving it
until the next sandstorm.)

Take, I think,
the green as it happens,
as we do not touch it
more than a foot press
on what grass we reach,
print, as it might,
mud or snow.
Use whatever senses may be left.
Always the touch
                    or the end
of touching.
Making sense of this,
draw smoke,
or as the old men
talking to the young
drop the stick,
that no one interrupt
the speaking.
Think of it carefully.
We are not here a long time.
We will not be here.
Shells and bones
that lives in seas
are on the peaks now,
may not be, tomorrow.

Fragile, how fragile we must be,
alone,
          or travelling.

Arapahoe

In strange country,
or just that midway—
by the apple tree,
between two places:
    poles.

XLIX

Something
        then
I would want to know
                or find—
if it were not there.
It is the heart-raising
             sense
that it is.
        That,
without looking,
I was able to find it
on a walk,
          where and when I had gone,
not, specifically,
to find anything,
or even feel much more
than the pleasure
            of kicking
footloose—
          through a few scant inches
of granular snow
           backed
by the dead leaves
of last summer.
I had companions
(not usual on such walks,
when delight is in going
             alone,
not being able to answer
            such questions

as,
　　　'Where you been?'
'What'd you see?'
(Perfect counterpart to
'How are you?'
　　　　　　Who cares?
I don't, and rarely say it.)
One of those things—
　　　　　　　taken—
nor do I want much
to get to the point
for a moment,
　　　　　　because
it tends to a direction—
a thinking—
　　　　　　perhaps Norse kenning,
if I were to use symbols,
and that is more important.
If I tell you
　　　　about things
which I know too well,
I am bored before I have finished.
And, if I tell you things
　　　　　　　　you
already know,
　　　　　you are bored,
even if I know less perfectly.
Why not discover it,
welcome, as the case is,
neither knowing
　　　　　　exactly where
the old road will go.
Grown up a bit,
　　　　　and then cut out
lately
　　to someone else's sense
of where it should go.
Nothing gets repeated
　　　　　　　evidently.
And I am not certain
　　　　　　either
that I want anyone more.
Three was not a crowd.

Creeley and Kline

Alison and Jake
wanted to come,
                    but
we left footprints—
perhaps too many.

Of Bert Mitchell's farm
-this one-
it has bounds more reasonable
than stake and witness tree.
It was laid out
when there was still enough land
to suit a man's whim:
to enclose all
                    of a particular kind.
(That the land owned itself,
and still does,
                    goes without saying.
It is possible,
                    merely,
to save a little of it
from the despoilers,
                    no matter
what guise they wear.
Brook Farm, and the
insurance men from Massachusetts,
                                    who hunt,
are equally
            unwelcome.)
That it made a district
must have been evident
to those who came here
                    earlier.

Among the usual tangle of new forest,
growing out of the nurse trees,
outcroppings
            raised
in little hillocks
with insistence /
                    / recurrence,
which I do not find
in other places in this town.

It is a joy to me
to find them
each fall when the leaves
are off again
to the bones of the hills.
Cairns,
            split rocks heaped
first by glaciers,
then split in recurrent
                        freeze and thaw.
Teeth and fangs,
                    saddles,
caves,
            crevasse and shale—
monuments ready to fall
                        over.
Sighting one of these,
                    we went on
to springs from a watershed
which ended the walking.

We climbed up there
on the return.
                    Moosewood,
in palings,
            around this one.
It was a place to rest.

Much later,
                    I thought of these places
again,
            and remembered the places
chosen by Icelanders
                    for assembly.
The 'thing.'
'Thing rocks?'
                    If I say so.
The story is all one
or various,
            as it may fit.
Touch
            something, then.

L

The man who wrote

               on my papers,
'taunt of presence.'

                  What did he mean
by that?

        Did he
write so—

            a notation for himself—
or something that I should see?
as later,

         I did see it,
faint and indistinct—

               a pencil scrawl
on one of the margins.
Was the man angry?
at me?

        at my work?
at himself for knowing
not enough,

           or too well?
It is a heavy sentence.
This happened many years ago,
does not disturb me often.
When it does, it

            works up
festers like

         an old wound,
or a splinter,

           wood or glass,
that surfaces,

          but won't come out.
a heavy sentence.
Do I think of him

          easily—
the man one called,

            'le beau garcon?'
He was not that gentle,
often sulked,
nor did he

        at times
believe in his own convictions.

Nobility encased in ice—
—the trap—
his fury burned no fuel.
Attempting and afraid,
at the same time standing,
an old prophet,
                    beside himself.
He could not touch anything
further than the taunt,
with which he mingled and misspelled:
Taint.
Why in this place,
or from this place?
I had forgotten it—
                    for years
looked elsewhere,
but all of it remains—
                    a part—
my/his story.
It works in—
                a difficulty—
something to infect and wound.
To pay for the healing?
other words
                others
wounds
            these days.

What to say—
when there is nothing—
nothing more than
saying—
            what the water
dripping from the eaves
may say.
It says to *me*,
neither of us at a loss.
It all is said:
as it once was,
as it is,
may, or will be,
what, or that,
                to say.

(Smudge of the sun,
snow before night,
kenning or reckoning—
cursed / blest.
Hard to come that way—
to go beyond it.

Where he came from?
Behind the hill—
'the high towering clouds of summer'
knew 'em well.
As the reprieve
                    ends,
and the pain returns—
looking out,
              the snow
that compasses or holds.
It will not end here,
flowing from the edge of spring,
under the hill downstream,
                              away,
washes
       words
or what they said.
A hardly spoken
                  flexion
parried.
Washed out in salt—
in metals
          gone as ice.
All that sounds
                  as all that flows,
seasons out of seasons.
How these angles cross.
Whereby.
As if there were answers
other than the run—
the taunt
taint of presence.
How it recurs.
Where I come back to it.
Spending myself
                  scant ways—

makes news of *that*
for credence.
It is the dark current,
                             it
moves on—
                   comes to
move itself,
                   no other moving—
no movement.

All day the wounded snow,
bleeding from the eaves.
Where did *that* come from?
How does it mean what it says?
A taunt in presence?
or presented?
(Earth taste in the drink of cider.)
The axis,
                spindle of return,
not sure,
Placed over the place,
the plans lie
somewhat apart.
Taken as trick—
spelled out—the devil hindmost,
or that part of him—
wondering—
worrying an old bone
for lack of sleep,
no meat for the taunt—
the holding place—
                             no taint.
Axis—
          and the earth taste.
Wholesome.
Measured by the day.
What was it? Heard?

(Daylight again—
the cutting edge—this light—
against a borrowed sense of it.
Or, as the light goes out,
to put some other on.

Lean these logs together,
that they burn up
for light from heat,
and let them be
sinking
            out.
The eye of the coal
as slip
            -misnomer-
eye of the cold—
bright, then glazed.
A brown eye
            into ash.
So many times to see these things,
the simple ones laid over,
or that voice—
            the hand that had it:
Taunt.
            As I make it,
accusation.
(Small warm places
in an outside cold,
wherever the life has settled
wearing a winter out.
Stasis as the blood clots thick.

Or it could be time to breathe
thin air—
turn nostril
            -flare-
and turn the flame.
Taunt?
It was unease
to be standing where I knew I did.
And this is the flex.
As if the knee or finger bent
of itself—
            the rest aloof—.
But this is not the way of it.
Lifeless in life,
without the center.
The taunt relaxes.
Disappears.

The small places—
warmth and fires.
Morning and evening lights
rise and arise—
fall with the coals,
rise again.
Fears burn out—
the fuel lowers.
Only a man remains,
breathing slowly
the high thin air.
The mists will cover—
the small ghost
of what might be,
and never would.

LI

Crowded
            against each other—
cheek by jowl—
nothing but men—
and why should we heed them?
They have not listened
to the old voices of the earth.
They do not care
                        to.

G.O.   "They do not like themselves enough."
And this is measure
of their failure.
The first to topple
dragging the others down.
Is that what we mean,
speaking of mankind?
His kind or his kin—
but kinship, surely a greater part
than this little—
familial, only to other men.

Leaning again, and the
first to topple
brings down the rest—
so much for strength or weakness.

"I warn you:
Man is the foe of the Old Life,
whether he knows it or not,
and in the end his works
will cover the world—
never again will it know freedom
or wild magics,
unless we bring him down,
haul him before it is too late
back into the brotherhood of
Beast, Tree and Waters."
Or standing alone at midnight,'
a horse's skull on a pole
pointed into Jutland.
The first to topple
will not be the last of them—
brings down the whole—
strikes fire in the sacred ash,
the binding rowan,
from which the Weird of the World—
sets fire to the bridge—
Ragnarok and darkness.
Crowded.
          Don't push.
In that push,
                speaking its progress,
lies the flaw.
And the toppling begins,
over and over.
We learn nothing,
eating the flesh of our own kind—
ignoring the story.
Sitting on bare tree,
whether it be good omen
                          or not:
A bird
      in thawing weather.

Skuld: Hrolf
Kraki's Saga

235

Or the quiet—
slight rain on the roof
close,
above the place where I work.
It is a good day
all in all—
only at a distance
the rumbling of that crowding.
What will topple?
Ice, perhaps,
through the first jams.
Holding on
                    this silence
as the day wears thin.

What of the seasons of men?
where they have supplanted
with locked-in fires,
the cold of the sun's distance
in winter?
That all should be flattened out
in sameness.
How can it be borne quietly?
Perhaps it would be good
to sleep under a log.
I have no solution.
(The horse skull points at me.)

Then after the work is completed,
it begins again.
There is no rest,
none asked for.
We would be hard put to it,
asking for other.
But there is greed of many sorts,
robbing one pocket to pay another.
The tragedy which has haunted us—.
Am I less now
than those others?
Trying to hold on,
well, that was augured
by an earlier master.
Shoring the walls

that nothing topple.
All down.
The weight of the winter.
Snow is small part of it,
to crack the ribs,
cave in, just before spring.
These are the hard seasons,
but we have made them hard.
No one to blame,
no place to give quarter,
or ask it.
Feeling the old wounds—
a twinge there—
wince—in the bone.
No way, but to go on
into the eye of the storm—
a momentary quiet.
Pleasure in some pain,
to go beyond the last sounds—
a quiet country—
moors and tors—
pool and tarn—
plash ponds, finally
the flow of the lost springs—
a vein of iron
caught by the sea.
Whatever is known,
was,
  swell of the tide
midocean—
    calm
until it strikes a rock,
skerry or islet,
lone, for the birds,
caught in sea rivers,
way and away.

And man,
   dependent upon what the rest made,
loses himself.
Will not come back,
the needle spinning

helpless to tell where.
A dark night to go down.

Nothing that takes itself
inside or out,
forced into pattern.
It occurs.
                    That is all.

Mention of high places
brought low,
covered with the smoke,
the remains of men,
even where the first grasses
thrust, and turn monuments,
gravestones unseated.
Cycles and centuries
to gentle the raw edges.
But the talk becomes aimless—
curses—
sows and sours the land with salt.
How may a man work there?
A carthaginian desert.
Even if he would go back
into the land,
his roots holding,
he may not.
Pariah in the waste
he has made for himself.
Concern and complaint.
The rust and the blood
flow far.
It is not easy to tell
one from the other.

LII

Do you, in any such place,
realize what you've done?
Self-congratulation
                              is
hardly a way to begin.
In several days I shall be leaving—
'shoving off' a good phrase for it,
as if I stood on the deck,
took my gaff,
and pushed against the wharf—
that it stay put,
to take the tide,
                              up or down,
accrue barnacles and mussels,
but that I should leave it,
enquiring for midstream.
I have sloughed another skin,
and that's another bit outworn
that goes into the shroud,
                              along with
several nails
              to batten down hatches
or other covers.
It is easy,
          or seems to be.

It is good to be in work,
and then to be beyond it.
For some of us, despite ill reasons,
there is no good, save the work itself.
A sharp-edged drink-
iced with alcohol—
but not what one adds,
                              rather
what the drink contains—
                                        has
from the cold around it.
Not that which is convivial.
I am not social in my habits,
only in my work.
and what I would,

                    for what I think
is good.
No reason to believe that—
much of it is not.
To find a little that coheres—
a few men of like mind.
I do not stand to embrace it all.
It *would* be folly.
Sadness that it can't be,
but what is not sad?
Not only men,
                    but weather—
in and out.
                    Ageing,
as a man becomes the younger for it.
Sad ness - sadness:
In the sun,
the sound of children,
and the seed.
Spring is bitter,
bread is bitter.
Live *in* bitterness,
do not become it.

What hand? not my hand,
has prompted this?
It does not burst in
                    or with rage,
but contains it—
the cloud the size of a fist,
nucleus to thunder.
And all say, 'gentle',
living in anything but gentleness.
It keeps rising,
dust devils on a dry field.
The day seems good.

This morning,
after a night of wind,
I come up that path
which links the two,
see scatterings of other lives—
the ghostly nexus:

                              milkweed,
spreading in the cold to fly—
old apples, brown as age,
twigs, leaves, pinecones.
Seed in the midst of death,
living in bitterness—
sweet—
                  and living.
Aha!
            Then it goes too fast.
None of us can find a place
where it does not go—
seeps into our clothes
                              like sand
pre-empts up.
                        Only an old man,
once,
asking for sleep,
where it did cohere,
even as he doubted it.
The days when it moves
as lead,
but those are the cold ones.
It melts /
                / is Phlegethon.
Abrades and wears away.
Too many times
we look away from it.
(Live bitterness,
                        rather
than in the bitter.
Touching and asking:
"We beg you sirs,"
if only for twice-used broth.
We do not need it—
but we fear.
I'd tried another way.
Slept in my clothes—.
The years to come back from that.
Trying for some poise—
leaning on an old man's cane.
And it *is* a harsh lesson,
my story,

E.P.

that I begin to know those terms:
SENECTITUDE,
a properly sonorous word.
Agh! Forget it.
To spit into the frost,
and hear the old bones crack.

They sometimes look in:
"Havin' a good time old boy?"
What am I supposed to answer?
'Of course (?) Damned right (?)'
Take it out of the songbooks—
eyes well enough to see them—
(or over the glasses—
the haze of far-off hills.
Is it:
'one day I'll be there.' (?)
'one day I was.' (?)
Provisional,
              but whom shall I
provision more?
I heard, one time in spring—
in summer—
brown hunting clothes—
It all sounds as cant.
I would avoid that.

              ★★★★★★★★★★★★

Which,
       at that point,
clears away the frames,
misconceptions, or the hill
before defeat.
All of it, the fear of an old man,
holds,
       like 3 a.m.
I put it so:
In the dead still
of the early morning—
that time when the pulse
drops
       lowest,

and the heart turns sluggish
and afriad—
        the all night lights
are ringed with brown—
dark circles,
        tired,
tired of the living,
          cold,
with an inside chill—
blank and waiting to wink out,
passed over by the day,
their formless shadows lost
as if
in waiting they were near,
So speaks despair,
or perhaps the hope
that this was darkest
Well enough to set it down.
Try living beyond it.
It is not self-pity,
nor much behind it.
it can be that anger,
taken from the body,
one body,
and given to the whole.
The rage at having come
this far,
        and seeing things
no different than once
through innocence.
           Ideals.
It *could not* change,
but that doesn't help.
Leaves his story:

mute
open

rage
spoken.

All things paired and coupled.
A street of pawn shops,
and men are dying on that street.

I wanted to ask one,
but they had no ears.
I doubt if they saw me,
doubled up in their own pain.
Convulsed,
                    yet I heard singing there.
It was not hell—
an ordinary city street.
I looked up and down—

St. Louis:
2/3/75

the sun trying to remake itself:
Reflections on a cloud—
giving back its life to itself—
no more monstrous than that.
(and one travelling with me
whistled a wordless
                    tuneless
tune.
I doubt if he saw that much,
his pawned soul
left on that street.
Earlier the shrill laughter
of poisoned women
making things ridiculous,
and no need to do it.
(Slight rain in the deserts,
the winter season.)
All so usual,
regular context.
I do not mind growing older
in such a place.
Give me return,
portion of it,
graps the mirror
to give myself life again.
Reflection has more heat
passing through glass.
I am climbing over detritus—
debris and skeletons,
but at sea,
returned to the land,
refined.
Some factories still going full blast.

It is not my intention.
No time for that.
Attention - then ?

LIII

Color of fawn's hide—
dappled to camouflage.
It breaks down,
opens fully.
The color of an ordinary day.
All that is needed:
                    this ordinary—
not much else—
and a grim sky,
                no rain,
hardly its throat.
Why do I say this?
There is no other experience
except my own.
No exaction.
I give my qualities to everything.
Midas touch
blackens eventually.
It is not hard to be genuine,
only if one works hard
to get the ring of the coinage.
Let it alone.
Blast hell out of hell,
not from anything other.
Color of fawn's hide,
and it would not be
unless I said it.
I have tried too hard
then.
There are not spaces
or trees.
            The pearls, deep down,

as pearls contain an imitation.
Well, it's ok to go on
like this, but it never
transposes back
through that great wheel of modulation,
similar, if not.
The circle of fifths.
Why not?
Why keep calling for it?
It is, on the surface,
an easier life,
alligned,
than what I knew.
All in the eye of beholding.
I behold.
       (Be held.)
No, you've got to remount,
remonstrate.
All of it color of a fawn's skin,
and hidden.
They told me a way to get on—
hideous, without face or forming,
I will not,
cannot take the substitute.
Several skins shed—
but at cost.
Blood and tissue open to the air?
They dry
        and do not breathe.
Buries the fawn skin.

I tried to look through the fog,
though it was in my own eyes.
(perhaps it was,
some of it was)
I could not move,
because of everything around me
                moving.
Encapsulated in it.
Coming along those green fields
to a pile of the red dirt
which grows them.
What do we know about colors?

Where are the congruents?
What makes them?

It is not the academic chart
of mixing one with the other.
I would say my fawn skin, grey,
and mottled,
has all colors in it—
possibilities of many more
we never saw.
Won't.
So my madness—
why, as I worm out of them?
(Looking for birds
in a swamp coppice.
The doves nest here.)
Cursed my own strength,
knew that had to happen,
and felt the side twinges,
afraid the joints would pull apart.
Spend some on full days.
That's the easiest way—
hold that color
as a line—
                color line?
An army or a fleet.
Always hardest
when its put that way.

Swinging the ring,
a circle or a pendulum—
might tell of children,
can't on the moving earth
stay still.
It's what I have come through,
what is through the color,
red earth, green grass,
grey fawn,
                dung,
the chain.
Wrestling with proportions,
open and over,
set in as fortune.

Stopping for an instant—
nucleus
        from which
ganglia.
Then turning again to ask,
if first thinking's best,
or any thought at all.
Flagging down the stops on that—
setting reeds.
We'll go along
            this
one day at a time.
I'll give it root,
and then the color.
Cannot tell the dark
from light.

LIV

Oh, Dr. Franklin,
I can't really admire you.
'Pappy', as I guess it's true
you were later
to your immediate family.
I'm not sure what all this
talk and veneration of
           'greatness'
leads to.
        You were the man
of that time,
          an age of curiosity,
and we've denied that
living on chrome and plastic,
              conceived
under Macdonald's Arches.
You were
        willing to live
a large slice at a time.

Inconceivable to sleep long.
Because of the interest in it,
life was interesting.
With what one uses:
the more of it
                    makes more.

Apparent
available
necessary.

But you were niggardly,
a shopkeeper more learned and skilled.
I might have liked you,
but kept my distance.
We would have talked of plants,
or that glass harmonica.
I might have hired you
to print a sequence.
But—.

No matter. It was the age,
more than any man.
A long time ago,
and that's like looking at
the folds of mountains,
not seeing the canyon
rising behind the wall:
Opens to high meadows
on the peaks.
Time
        and the man,
or timing in the man
-a timing- held to the ear-
a tone—sound of it.
Without that there is nothing,
and no man.
Heaping its substance,
as it breathes
                    through.
Dr. Franklin, you were subject,
you and Mesmer,
                    even Mozart,
though that was clearer,

South End, Organ
Mountains
2/8/75

249

the fate of genius,
whatever genius makes
or is.
Excitement and enthusiasm,
those sharp edges,
how they conspire
to true an edge.
The air is clear,
and it is morning,
perhaps October,
fruition before a lapse
or sleep.

It is all too easy to reconstruct
what we have no sense of
living in it.
Nor do I think your life that easy.
You believed,
had the pivot there.
That is more than the rest of it.
But I could not have liked
the haggling over business—
money as the power.
That you loved men is apparent,
I am grateful,
              as I must be;
yet I sense a taste
for notoreity—
that you gave nothing for nothing,
nor would I open shop each morning.
You had the tools,
were the workman.
It would be hard to say more of it.
Could you have taken time
to rejoice in failure,
you,
      and your compeers,
I would be happier.
A mixed life,
as it was a mixed breed
that fashioned those several early states.
It is good to be involved,
better, to know why.

The maxims and metaphors—
well, they *are* curiosae,
and I suppose to be preserved.
Dr. Franklin, we are getting on,
most, in the denial,
out of those years
                    when both of us,
as all men,
did things well through inexperience.
An old man loses nerve
if he depends on thinking.
I remember myself,
                    cautiously,
coming down over the shale slope.
And the man at the bottom:
"I guess it *is* hard,
now that I think about it.
I just came down
                    without thinking."
Possibly diplomacy would be better
without the plan.
The dark stain of intrigue
is everywhere on it.
Well, grasp it,
don't.
We do go on,
and you and I, at several hundred years
remove, may get on
famously.
            (A just and English word)
Or, if it can be in words
                    at all?
I sometimes think not,
and making mention of our acknowledged
'great'men,
            poke a hole
in the entire structure.
Peremptory decision—
this for this,
            or that,
or nothing,
            and the owls,

raccoons,
         more feral
through the weak and rotting straws
of winter.
         The while this 'greatness'
lies under a stone
           near a restaurant
in Philadelphia.
I am not demeaning it—
merely
       wondering—
as in my own case.
Well, it's all a case
of history.
The repository of some other sounds.
Little I can tell
         further.
Pappy, I feel strengthened,
in that you
      as I
had eyes for pretty girls,
and sometimes more.
The great activities?
Well,
     we can't put those
in one category.
Dr. Franklin,
         whatever the abuses
of that power,
       you *were,*
and you repeated:
"Without it, there is nothing,
and no man."

LV

RK

Sleep, as a simple stone,
to sleep *that* way—
'tomorrow is possible

                                  because it is.'

the way
           and I do not
live well without the dreams.
At any rate, a night—
night in which I slept well,
a short night,

                 possibly the best.

In which 'Owen'

             and 'Barstow'

figure—

          the antecedent name,
a town in California—
how to link them—
as all things must be linked.

G.Q. 2/24/75

(Of course, there was *Barfield*—
but at this point of what use to me?
At another time.

                I *slept*

well.
Always the sexual connotations:
no matter how,

            where,

Dream, 2/25/75

or the impossible connections:
There is nothing that cannot contain the earth,
and if there is,
more than suspect.
to retain and reify
by that mountain alcohol
overproofed.
The only strength one can contain.
I spend

       mere
         time.

              But time on all its levels.

The japanese servant boiling water
for his cup of tea,

while I am set upon
other fortunes—
living through several, if not many,
lifetimes.
(Can't cut what has length in my direction.)
Oh yes,
to think about it,
but the thinking is no better,
and apart from an occasional headbreak.
All I've had from it—
some broken bones.

Kipnis, as
Godounov

The heavy man falling
down a flight of stairs—
"Bozhe. Bozhe moi."
They can't commute the sentence,
even if the sentence is not given.
The lives flow out.
They keep on coming.
?going?
We've tried to put it into sense,
sense not being (always)
context.
(That the bed is a good one
-hard enough-
              by cold window
to sleep well there.
Woke refreshed.
No one can deny that much,
though many will try it. ·
Whatever a man writes,
he does it oiut of
his simple context.
HUM DROM,
that is not flattened.
Not losing.
Nor simple.
One *has* to deal
with the complexities of breathing.
It is *not* sick to say,
as one, :
but I think he did.
There are many concerns

we can't get into.
This fear of 'au courant'.
I have never yet seen stream or snow
that did not flow.
I am filling it up—
all up with ink tracks—
pay attention to the white spaces
flowing.
It's that way—simple.
Most of us
won't read another poem—
some fear in that delight.
Or the simple fallen stone—
that sleep—
                    in
tensing.
               The terse word.
How it leaves a man
looking for a hand up,
or down,
careful,
no matter what:
the leap.
However I involve myself
in it
or around it—
I'm taken further
from the point—
RK* Annandale,   which was, that I lay here
February, 1975   on a good bed—
surprisingly good—
(used to my own)
and I slept well,
the window open
to the thaw—
the last ice patches—
early spring.
And I thought in terms of space,
that it was between,
and not those objects:
Smaller   "Form is emptiness, and
Pragna-Paramita   emptiness is form.
(trans. Max Müller)   Emptiness is not different from form;

255

form is not different from emptiness."—
"(The seeker) becomes free from all fear,
and beyond the reach of change—."
Or perhaps I had not reached,
lived on the edge,
where I may have gone since:
That darkness where I fear
voidance.
Of grim days,
well, *what* of them?
I am asking questions,
used only to the answers,
where only the questions suffice.
It was more than that.
I slept.
Nothing from nothing.
What is—
seems to be.

I was not clever,
          early on,
only late that I discovered
what it was I wanted to do,
or how to say it,
since that doing has implied
other than physical moving.
What has come
          has been of dream,
the darkness of mystery
suddenly lighted.
In the mishaps
          I have found it,
the misreadings.
          Slips of speech.
As he said,
          thining of what was close
to him,
          and lost,
'At the time of our death.'
No more than that.
The great concerns do not apply.
and it is better to go
               once

to a good bed
                    than read late.
Much more to say?
It will not be so much the words,
as the spaces
                    around them—
penumbra, and shadow
proper.
It was not for anything
save that which prompted,
'great within us'
and burst out—
if no more than an old wound,
ugly and festering.
We do not know how
or where this is—
how it was,
                    except by blood.
Sucking the venom out,
it will not all be lost
or spit away
                    into the dust.

So I had slept,
quietly enough.
It was hard to get up
into the morning—
                    only because
I willed it.
Refreshed, I did not yet
wish to leave the source—
then did—
sat quietly in sunlight
at the kitchen table.
It was good to be there,
                    too.

LVI

?——me fecit.
What it was,
                    now lost.
Some dolor or doom,
no doubt of that.
Why shouold I imagine further?
What comes unbidden
may or may not stay on.
Counting butterflies,
                              they soon
transpire—
                    nor do they eat
in that slight passing.
There is little luck.
We do not read of it
as permanent.
Nor can we touch there.
Days so spent,
                    nights in recall—
the other levels fallen
through.

I stood looking
(myself around me)
at the day.
This morning-
                    —fecit?
That ice which dropped in showers
from the trees.
'When I am buried, who will be alone?'
(—me fecit?)
Any poet
              in his voice of passion.
An old memory—
                          old thing
dredged up imperfectly,
leaving the rust on,
                              some of the solids
undersea.
              It *is* a long time
walking there—

Linda Shoyo

258

                   under-
me fecit.
Then the days buried
along with old armor,
bowls of food,
that the dead may journey with it.
I remember
                   -poorly-
whatever threadbare selves—
oh,
take it for what it was,
don't ask me
anymore.
                   But I have given
the heart over—
it will rise again.
Never broken—
                   this ring of knowing.
Full—a prophecy—
taken out of living—
not the artifact—
                   me fecit.

Tempted by logic,
resist it.
This morning clears,
these fields—
                   that
swell of snow,
the curve of shoulder,
breast or buttock—
how the hill holds
-did not make it-
feminine. The thrust
is air.
(Sound—dry boards cracking—
is it that?
are any days such days
as spend themselves on brittle sound?
Look to something else,
                   if only
the artifact—
only the rhythm of the sounding

set against wind
for silence.

Then—
          as it all wears out—
a man can rise
-if that is what he does-
up in the morning
to do whatever his hand
or eyes
          -whatever—
he may do
          or know.
Me fecit.
Bring it on—
the time is light again.
All that is most glad—
most dangerous.
What it is to
rearrange it.

Mentioning the sense,
one has the thrust—
is had.
How much?
and with the heterodyne
of other talk.
Who does the talking.
What is it - makes?
When this time creates,
it touches me.
My hand releases,
as the tools falls down—
me fecit.
Not always the conscious act.
What "gleaming dagger?"
Something points.
It carries out
at that point,
or what I make the point.

The doodles—
what I can't draw—
tense pictures.

Lieder Eines
Fahrenden Gessellen

Facio, facere, feci, factus.
I can't read anymore:
a fault of glasses,
late at night,
that I may listen—
not work,
under
          "darkening shingles,
blackening rain—"
where did *that* come from?
Never knowing
harsh corrections—
the status
          station
not to be kept
                    longer.
Looked at the service—
all quiet there.
Nearly flew out of my skin—
why does it abrade?
Weather and circumstance
glued together—
a hard day to leave.
Hence making,
turned inside the dream.
Place of the—

          feci?

LVII

If a stroke is in the wind,
go find it—
how it places touch
against the ear
                    and
makes it feel the sound
before it opens.
                    Ice click

-rattling bones-
                    the lithe cane
knobbed—
            buds broken.
Sound that reaches color,
push and taste.
It opens carefully.
Pain and joy—
                    this sound cuts deep.
The ordinary things recede—
its opening
the wave that cannot stop.
Go find it

Now—in this pleasure—
that the day is clear again,
something required
long lost.
The man might look for them—
the high sun over him.
Wind slack—
sound gone down.
(Catkins breaking over snow—
soft sound
                slip of a season
melting into another.
Smother and muffle—
thick as wool
                    the rotten ice
downstream.
                    Surge and flow.
Yellow as leaves,
                        measured dilution—
it flows away.
At night it hardens.
Stroke again—
                tap of the wind—
the senses split apart.
Reassemble.
                    To remake them,
stroke on tap—
                    on tap—   —
tap   -.

Wherever the wind is large enough,
go find it.
Little more than the despair,
the winter leavings.
Long, so long,
feet soaked in ice,
water and slush.
Hot flaring sun overhead
turns a man blind,
snow blindness—
that sound.
A longer way—
the one which opens
from doors—
                    the closest ones—
goes journies
which distances deny.
A fullness,
something held,
                    then
given back.
Why does it all preform?
A warm spring morning
after bitter night.
(The tongue will stick
on frozen iron.
Those days of ferment,
when the senses,
                    dizzying,
come steady—
clear again.
(As if the earth were rising,
thinning from beneath—
emergent sound,
                    tactile,
the *breath* that clears,
will lighten.
(Tap in the wind,
a stroke-
           tap—
Free and away.
Ice at the edge
           reformed.

Places where the voice
must end.
I have found them—   .
looking for other sound.
Some will come
                    -wholly :

4/14/75

As on that day,
climbing the hill,
surrounded by it,
feeling its heat,
its strangeness,
as if it came
from something other,
not this world.
Go there ?
It will come.
The sounds are in itself.
Nothing to be had
                    further.
Who will know it ?
Where did I ?
In what life ?
More than the dream,
blackness left—
a hole in the bright day—
its passing.
Thinking of that
go on.
But the strength
loses force.
No will.
Climbing, bent,
what was it ?
Why did I come here ?
Some ordinary act,
picking up stones
or wood.
Sound of a tree
                    falling
somewhere cut down.
Sound cut off.
This, as always,
the way in and out.

If you look for a path,
you will not find it.
Go in - as go on -
by some inkling,
placed in the bones.
That knowing.
May have fallen down,
here and in other places.
The witness,
                and the witness tree.
Mute reproach.
A pile of rubble,
lasting longer—
that delight
                this sound.
Come here
                that I hear it
-tap in the wind-
struck in the wind.
On a night,
of a far night's passing,
through
                and out.

LVIII

This the enemy
who will
                sweet talk
his way into and unto you,
or to me.
                He will smile
that superior grace
                                as if he knew
'better' than what?
He will have reasons,
text and canon,
                and

he will never change.
He will smile—
                    not know his deceit—
it is sad.
            He does not know
the enmity he bears,
but thinks of his way
as the only one,
sanctioned by useage,
hermetics, cut off from change.
And he is everywhere,
sitting in council and judgement,
learned in the uses
of the past—
                    using the past,
as the past was never like that,
takes on a taint of morality,
and foreshortened distance.
He is the enemy,
and the man with whom
we drink tea in the morning,
gin in the late afternoon.
He does not know
what he is saying,
closed fist and closed mind,
nor that the past he structures
was not that past at all—
he has given 'history'
but not his story.
He is contemptuous,
                    devoted
to memorabilia,
biography,
            the memorable line.
A form imposed
            and played out,
logically, to prescribed limit.
He is neat and precise.
It is a game with him,
and he has never heard of life.
If he is sad,
it is sadness calculated
for its effect.

His library is intact—
unread.
The systems he evolves
are complete—
the snake swallows its tail,
and there is no sign of join.
His means are not simple,
unless he can fake them,
and he knows nothing of this,
believes he is loved,
imperishable.
Into and unto—
all things to all men.

(As the flow of the wind
was a wind unjoined—
the gale's flow,
force and a witless scream,
yet centered
                and making
a form out of void.
It could be felt,
understood—
the bands of light air
about me
            then burst.
The light was around me—
the day had no boundaries
except for its own :
that day.

And the enemy believes,
he believes in progress,
and goals—
gives to the community chest.
Swells with pride,
when the thermometer rises—
the amount is received.
He talks of suffering,
as if he had suffered,
who has never scratched the surface
of agony, nor
yet seen blood.

He talks of birth pangs,
but cannot give birth.
All drops
        cold as a stone.
He would like to talk,
tells anecdotes—
listens for applause,
some of which he has.
He is satisfied.
I can't talk to him.
He sees my anger,
takes it for something else.
We pass each other
poles apart,
each with his partisans.
I have met the enemy.
I am disappointed in his steel.

(And the light of the evening
stays long,
over the flaccid heaps,
old slush,
the stalks and scapes
-last years'—
dissolving in water.
The light of the sky,
late,
falling into place,
disjointed
when seen on edge,
but a whole,
made all in all.

The enemy,
glib in his teaching,
is always willing
to teach,
and at great length.
The theory is his,
but he is hard put
to find more than that.
There is nothing specific.
He scoffs at intuition.

It must be hammered
at his forge.
When he is cornered
he will scratch and bite.
Kick below the belt.
He has told me
what he thinks of those
who work in other places
than his own:
"It can't be worth very much."
He has a smile
which he thinks of as
enigmatic.
He thinks to kill with it.
Medusa or basilisk.
Frail heat.
He dies on the way.

When his master,
the greater man,
changes face,
        sees
something that is now
to be seen,
was,
     simply
what was not available,
the enemy reshuffles his cards
for whatever trumps remain.
It is hard for him,
but he must not be found
lacking
       or unfashionable.
He forgets all
but imagined slights.

(Turning dark,
now is the time to gamble
with strengths and warmth—
to test the unseen love.
To cool angers—
that the heart opens,
does not harden.

The quick of it—
largesse.
What has been given?
Nothing that will stay.

The enemy?
A long time ago
he was here.
Later, a few cerements.
Ashes.
His story.
    Dust.

LIX

Bell from the
Grunewald foundry.
Symphony #2, 1896

Quinine, the first
'proving', 1790

Mahler's bell—
before it sounded,
Hahnemann's cinchona
or reverse.
The stream is the same.
Few go there,
those who do,
bring back a story
of far country, farther dream.
All of this dreaming
holding onto my own hands
as if they were the only ones
-true guides—
yet I know them
                not to be.
How a man might think of form
as flow,
never a recapitulate—
nothing quite the same.
The virgin repeats,
and that is the answer,
if it is need, or wanted,
usually not.

at Grunewald

"The cold did me good,
as I had spent another sleepless night."
(Bell tempered by what air?
To find what is needed
is to stretch out the hand—
or a sense that can take it in)
As it was?
Is it *not*?

(Light airs stirring,
or rough edges,
a hoarse day,
as if it had caught cold
standing in slush.
As that swift violence
which comes again and again,
the morning between beats,
when the snow falls thick
and obscures the guideposts.
It is that darkness,
indecisive,
          the grey clouds
frozen again—
and the seed in them—also
frozen.
I am choked on what I desire,
walking out to the south,
and the direction of sunlight.

It is not—
we can go back
only in thinking—
the darkness has kindled
a light of its own.
And many days—
the lights of those days,
standing in darkness—
the seed in a stone
which will burst it.

Later, another man tried,
thinking to rest
a false concept.

Constantine Hering
(c. 1820)

Bought barks of one
who feared for his life,
or his reason.
He survived.
Is there more one could say?
It seems the left hand side,
where the road lies in shadow,
the snow stays longest,
and the earth, cool enough
to grow
                when the rest is dust.
An enclosure away
                    from the storm,
but not too easy.
The fingers pinched
to keep from going numb.
No one reaches
                back and forward,
tense giving
sound of that bell.
(Mood come upon me—
only the day itself
to answer.
Can I say—or sing—
or reach or strike?
Empty or full—
the shadows' passing.
And the flow of the wind,
a wind unjoined.
In all these places
I am able to turn,
and turn again,
though it is light air stirring,
or the flow of wind.
                    I face,
and rarely fall to face
full in.
The eyes of it—
take care—the eyes
relive the dangers
of the past.
They will not leave,
or let go easily.

Samuel Hahnemann
(c. 1785)

A man in his own fury,
working,
        scarcely knowing
days from nights, but able,
-as in the hut-
working two nights at a stretch
in a cloud of tobacco smoke—
only a curtain from those who slept
and could not understand him.
Or others,
        so many others
contained in the work,
a prison, as a freedom.
They do not reverse.
There is no route to understanding
unless the man is there.
It can be explained,
nod of assent
-even help- but it is resented,
and inthe end
the man stands alone,
left alone,
nothing more inside him.
There is this as cautionary.
The left hand road leads
among thorns.

(Power of the wind,
or the eyes—
        mine, at the winds'
looking far enough
over the north ridges—
the mist of a coming snow.
or is it centered there?
Our fears go higher
than our hopes.
The wind stiffens in ridges.
Cold remains,
        always the steel,
wherever the sun leaves
or cannot reach.
        The glowing coal
that turns in upon itself-

smaller-
        yet divine   rage.
Held up—
a leaf in the hand.

The bells,
        ringing
the sense
        strengthened.
The power
        and the eye.

LX

Those moments
        one after another
(surrounded by sleep
that the others dream
        quietly—
lending their concentration.
It becomes an occupied silence,
in which the vision
clears of its own pregnancy.)
Dreaming there,
        I rise
into the moment—
        as the concept
-moment prefigured-
        was exact.
Whatever I had in hand,
the exact / split.
It is never possible to go
far beyond it,
yet the day springs fully armed
from this as dyad :
the male and female deity.
It is hard to say.
Bound or cut off?
Not a likelihood.

274

Concerns - other -
mundane or humdrum,
lock themselves into it.
It is the printer's quoin
tightened and set up.
Many days, their continuities
foreshortened.
It is, indeed, the moment.

(Nor as I read much of it
                        at one time—
the moments will not come true
if they are faced.
They have their own context,
and there is nothing more
that can be done with them:
Wayward
            not willful.
Their own ways
                    not for bargain.

All this, which concerns me,
let it open out
into the single moment.
Let it come down
(voice that is hortatory—
may it quietly
                    subside,
whatever here
                    is its own decision.
Every day is its weakness
the point / decision,
strength as the moment.
Only the abstruse comment
where the hero lays about him
-hewing-
            that bright sword.
Decision rises—
flickers / out.
Bend of the eye
or cone of light.

What I once knew:
                    white heat—
blood for hematite—
a stone.
Congealed - the fire prisoned -
held inside
                    waiting.
Moment as sheer time—
weight of time—
what one might take in hand,
sense the latent,
or let it be.
Once I had heard such music
as the language held—
its prisoning,
precision,
                    the simultaneous
                                        moment:

"The sound . . . . . of a word
never apart from its meaning."
A´rising inflection,
falling from the scale,
placed as heights and depths,
seized on the moment.
Where it is required,
a regimen.
one after another—
as likely superimposed.
The ice / the reflection.
All that holds is water
as the water changes.
Pierced—
as itself.
Or in itself doth rise
the next surprise.

Pith or the pit
hard as a stone—
the marrow of seed.
Let that suffice
for moment—or as momente—
stand alone.
It is more than a possibility—

a giving and taking—
opening or unbuttoned—
flattened as ripe fruit,
not far from the burst
into the moment.
(or the sore with the infection
breaks the same way.)
Yet there is magic in it,
always enough magic—
what is ripeness
                    what corruption.
There are choices offered
which one does not choose—
lies open to the moment.
Seems as if the doors closed—
slammed shut—
broke a few fingers in the process.
Then opened of their own accord—
no pressures,
                    the moment
is all of it.
As it might come through
a broken window—
light for the day—
sound for the night
in flood season,
the last snows of the mountains
melting away.
                    (Streams at high tide)
or a look upward
11/14/74/ - 4/30/75   at take from reach
the moment grafted to another,
no time between.
Whatever shines-
                    shines out-
old metal,
                    broken glass,
harness buckle
                    -the like-
or a stone.
A chorus makes from it.
Can we reach sound!

OBSERVE the color—
the attempt.

An ascent - a warmth
in such cold.
Little to be said of it—
trial, always the trial—
whatever ends.
or the moment, unknown—
opening itself to guess
or question.
Not to be found there—
hardly known before it is gone—
winks out again.
May hammer
            its suggestion
the querulous tap of a bird
at the windows—
seeing through—
impatient that it may not come.
Always the moment
as the moment is not.
As if—
            trails off
that question.
Looks back on itself,
but not as we look for it.
The sound of one coming,
but not coming here.
There are no roads open,
and the way is choked.
Merely to accept it—
flow of the moments
as moments come—
and will.

LXI

So dear - so close —
the sounds of morning
clear around me
bird for bird,
that territorial right declared
before the dew is off,
the last cold eddies
of the night
given over to the sun.
So dear - so close -
the copyist assays it,
sets it down.
The copyist who lies—
bah!
why say it this way?
'lieblich'
said before,
               and yet
what else to say?
and who will say it—
generations ripe—
they fall away.
So dear - so close -
the sounds of morning.
A child sits in the sunlight
waiting—
               I take this time
to write it down :
a sometime copyist.
The first approach—
a damp and deep of morning—
closeness—
how the air smells—
light and cold—
promise of a long hot day—
now, briefly,
I tighten
               myself
and what I feel to be myself,
tending on smoke
the early kitchen fire.

Woods Hill—
spring, 1975

5/15/75

279

Few may know these things themselves—
we all remember
                        in the blood.
Is it fortune?
                        maudlin?
or nostalgia?
The close in such silence.
Let the others sleep,
and let me hold on here.
I know so little of the past—
yet know it all.
I open, budding,
as the shadbush—
amelanchier, and another spring.
Cutting a way through silence,
yet containing it.
No footprint.
Let it all shake out—
tighten the blade.
One last cup of tea.
Into the woods.
The concerns of the day.

Think small,
and work it—
                        small.
In sudden silence—
to eke that out—
to feel it coming
against me
through the open window.
'Pollen float from star is fatal,'
as an old musician said.
The dust and motes—
particles of the years—
so dear - so close.
Redundant.
What is that?
Here, nothing can repeat
or be repeated.
We think too often—
our impatience.

Conrad Aiken

280

(Dry trickle—
                    dust will fall—
the fatal pollen.)
Waiting to fill these patterns—
only a footprint in the muck,
filling, later, with water.
Shower - Shower
wind and shower—
water—what?
They come - they bring -
                              what?

Fill up and fly,
frequent and die —
high dizziness, the speech,
the melody gone long ago.
Sagging beams and rusted nails—
they left full long ago.
The ghosts -
                    oh -
shower - shower —
cannot sing—
slips down the dust.
(The man told me,
'Be happy in your work.'
And I listened, knowing
that he had granted
a great gift.
So dear, so close,
so very close—
sing on and off the key.
Day, that I should rise the most.
Is it nothing more
than getting up and getting down?
Who listens anymore?
Who has seen me?
Deep days, and dark days,
under the trees—
under the leaves long past—
the snows gone by.
reach me.
            One last cup.
The morning's clear,
and I am out.

281

LXII

Whatever he thought,
watching me as I embraced
the trees,
it was in far country from mine.
He was unhappy,
silent after several days.
He didn't know me,
never had.
I knew this, and warned him
at the outset.
"Stay away, you won't like it.
Things are different.
If I choose colors for the sky
I make them stick.
Bent on my own drumhead."
(But if I
          lost those trees?)

I remember the story
of two brothers,
lacemakers and
dealers in lace.
They were old men already,
living in the loft
where they had worked together
for many years.
Lace was no longer popular,
and the two old men
sat sadly, night after night,
over cold cups of tea.
Finally, apparently with few words,
they made a pact—
left a note on their worktable,
joined hands,
and jumped four storeys
to the street.

(If I lose those trees?
Even now, I hear a light wind
stirring them.
The wind where I am,

many miles away,
may reach them.
There are those who
do not care for such things,
who still laugh,
as that man,
                    many years ago.

The order of impressions here,
so far from that.
The sounds of early morning,
growing into day,
that far walk downtown—
the whores who ask me
if I'd like
                'to go out, love.'
I *am* out, and far beyond
them, or the rest of them,
butchering and curing
                        other meat.
I am alone this day,
free to put together all
I can find.
Free? yes,
            abroad.
And from other trees, those,
three in their row,
as natural a plant
as may have come to them—
years on—
the silent flow—
runnels each spring—
the snow
            falls / down.
As foreign as the sounds
of other words—
plain speech—no doubt—
exotic to my ears.
Well, play it down,
and don't forget the trees.

Marble Cemetery
N.Y. 5/28/75

A man will stand
against a wall
-full sun-

the shade inside,
imprisoned there,
as he is,
loss of will, perhaps.
of loss more simple.
Dark times, and known
before I knew them.
A simple bee or ant
is not at variance.
Look at us.

All these times, then,
come together,
not run-on
-rainsoaked colors-
simple, accurate,
their own shapes
in their own time.
Not popular.
Well, the populace
will come again.
They'll want that lace.
Oh, if I had lost those trees,
how much time I'd waste
finding them again.
Fashions, but fashions are
only multifacets of things
which do not change—
now one,
        and now another
picking up the light.
We all must go on—
thread the streams
up to the headwaters—
further—
to the least sign of dampness
into the source.
Into the blaze of will,
that source,
where will is gentle /
entire.
Trees catching light.
Hold on.
        Hold on there.

LXIII

Somapoetics 57

"—Call it a call in a stump
and leave it at that."
(George calls it 'Mrof',
and I do not know it better,
or a better way.
The echo of form—
the clod given shape
in air—
    the aethers.
Puff of smoke, that far.
Echo.
    Brass (mit dämpfer.)
But you can't turn it around,
which is a round
in all places,
is not backwards,
twirling,
    in / out / around.
Or as they say here,
straightening to the echo
or the beginning:
'righted around.'
The language holds it,
and we've not learned it
from objects—
aimless symetrics
tried on—
    tried out.
Tired— the dirte—
Something
    (ohne dämpfer)
full and tutti
parallel(s)
    para:
around.
    The canon.
Mixed with greed.
(muffled the reed)
Tension
    flex

iron—
          the heat
to that degree
laser let through—
that sharpness.
 Ha!
          climb down,
holding to the shoulder
on
     on soldier
no / on / one.
Fire.
          Well, he had it
for the stump,
from stump—
stump or branchwater,
good for the differences.
The darkness.
The dead. derring / do—
erring - o
soft and oft
cut off.

Now I think you might come out somewhere on the other side of the
echo.

LXIV

μνημοσύνη —
                    the Dorian—
from which
          to which,
and thereby remembrance.
What he *says* to me,
and yet the details blur
most in certainty.
How will a man proceed?
As it strengthens,
                    focus,

(foreshortened)
                              the large design
            left behind at times.
            The unobtained.

Gustav Mahler: Bear it in mind:
Maiernigg,   "—that which one desires in youth, one attains to later on."
Summer 1901

            All of these things forgotten,
            and that memory
                              in certain places
            plays us false.
                              It should.
            A bad memory plays
                              no tricks.
            It leads into other places,
                              builds new lives.
            Yet there are moments—.
            Mnemosyne! Mnemosyne!
            I should retrain myself
                              to remember.
            Cold—
                  blown in from the sea—
            even in late season,
                              crisp
            as the young leaves
                              in a garden under rain.
            It is true we have no home there,
            but a place
            to set out from.
                        Never ignore
            the place of origin.
                        The root,
            transplanted,
                        still feels a hold,
            a nerve,
                  throbbing.
            Where it once was.
            Homeground-litoral-
            the tide's edge.

            (As the cold draws on,
            continues, even in the sun,
                              full face,

                                                  287

it blows stiff
out of the north.
                    I am sitting
in that silence—
                         a slight protection
drawing in enough warmth.
I am at peace with it.
Worlds away—
the dreaming memory.
Making of it— —
not much to make.
The place I had always wanted—
here,
        at last.

Who finds it out, and
what
      is it?
We go through motions,
courtesies which are no more—
windows opening on walls.
It is in other places—
those places lost
                  unless—
recall—?

(And mother of the muses—
to have held that much:
hearing and movement,
                    sight
and the joy in sorrow.
That one for his story.
Taking the lightness,
pain on pain.
The wet adheres—
a dry sound.
Who mentions it?
Comes unasked for—
is a memory.
I lie alone.
Fortunate, that morning,
or the night after it.

Snap of the metal,
straightening /
                    settling
in the sun.
Remembrance of - what?
Each day
              stretching the muscles
back to something—
or here?
Hard to keep the tenses straight.
or strength—
this tensile—

Threading a way through—
aisles of it—
not all dark nor obscure—
some in light,
or where the distance
is reflected closer—
mirage—
that waiting on.
Holding up the dam—
one leaf—
the deluge comng one day—
a leak
tearing the roots and the sockets,
rocks and their memories,
notions gone downstream.
The lines grow sharper:
What one desired is had,
perhaps not wanted.

That rain!
          Again—
a new rain,
              or elder—
what do I remember
rain on rain?
Last week, or last aeon.
This bone that holds me—
upright—
mine? a new bone?
Or a crutch?

What did it hold before?
The tricks of memory,
as the poor one:
How we go on.

But then a dream
which is timeless,
rather, time-consumed.
Is there no memory?

Gorki: Bystander   Or is it that story?
"Was it a boy?
Perhaps no boy at all."
The float together,
times that interact.
I *think* I know—
memory, as preface,
trails off here.
Light in the leaves,
raised in darkness,
reflected in a blowing wind,
late at night—
another's light—
another distance—
consciousness exposed.
Raw nerve.
Echo, reflection, photograph—
all memory,
and I do not like what I see
in proofs,
          or in a mirror,
unless the mirror is indistinct.
Poor memory,
a memory without the fact—
that's what I'm getting at
or looking for.
Perhaps one day—?
Trails off again.
But in these ways,
to find the story—
the fee simple, underlying it.
And it is stupid to talk
of truth or falsehood:
As it was.
          Who cares?

Is is now
        as / is / was.
The wind in the leaves again.

But, gently!
In the morning,
even a grey morning,
well, and well-disposed,
the mind, open—drifting—
the means are there.
It does not *do* to wonder.
Day, full and fresh.
It is enough.
It is no time for scholars of the past.
The young man sets
himself to it—
holds the reins—
or did.
There is a music
in the quantity of sound
and air.
He will, hardly, need more than
his hand—
        what his hand finds
before him.
The mists rise later.
Perhaps he will have gone
into the fields by then—
soaked himself in dew.
It won't be long now—.
What?
The doubt creeps in—.
(there *were* those leaves
in the wind and light—
patterns crossing and recrossing
across the wall last night.
Lead him on a bit—
let him remember.
It is mine, Mnemosyne.
All I see is mine.

End Second Book

Book III

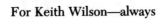

For Keith Wilson—always

LXV

The sea! The sea!
θαλαττα
                    but the return,
two as one—
                    no division,
the inner lands,
                    still.
Break of the first edges—
along the line—
                    sight—
nothing to be seen,
or nothing to see—
eye formed in water,
the water itself.

Mahler: notation at   As at the end,
the end of sketches of the broken instrument.
Symphony # 10   The means from which we were,
to which we are,
                    become
in such a moment—
as dissolved—
                    suspension—
sea and sea again.
The high-girt islands—
stone and wash—
sound—breaking sound.
The inner and outer passages.
Sailing clean against
(or in) the wind
                    its irons.
"Leb' wohl, Leb' wohl,

ibid.   Mein Saitenspiel"
The loosening—
                    the hold
on other means.
It rises, fades.
Fire /
        ice / blue.
I do not hear.
        I hear too well.

Wind that stiffens from the south,
props up the wet,
but does not freshen.
World, or where we are in world—
an understorey in the sea.
Elements that surround us,
sweep us down—
that silence,
tension,
            and the wind again.

Cannot hold it
                in the scale of notes.
It goes beyond
or off another way.
It hardly breaks,
breaks open.
Listen
        care
ful
    rises measure.
And the sea springs up.
Its tide is over
                whelmed—
turns brackish to the lees.

They never sing?
Or they never sing *there*?
here?
            the locus?
Do they sing?
Who will permit the song?
the song that rises on the wind?
or falls away to darkness?
(triplet and quarter note—
darkness
        following.
Sweet wet of the night.)
Or the song:
'thrown out of a rainbow.'
A child says that,
knowing lineage.
Where will the song

Hermit thrush

come from ?
                    Where will it go ?
And who permits
what is to be ?
Let us sing
further and further.
Let us climb to singing—
let us *be*
              to sing.
*The lovers—***how** *they* sing.

Apparent and permitted :
These rocks that sing.

Possibly because we
do not sing
the rocks
              have us.
But the rocks
                    do sing.
the sound
              of rocks
in rain or silence,
drought or distance—
Chrrrr !
              the bird.
We who do
are all.
SING
SING!!

In the end,
              if you die,
you know where you die.
You *will* know.
                    I, too.
All do not.
Pity—pity pushed offshore,
Voice, and voices
                    raised.
How soft the loudest clamor
-stroke and hammer-
                    stroke,
drum beyond the beat of drum.

Pity —pity,
              end and end.
The night springs up—
day springs
              up
  and down.
              The sea
  -voice-
          outside
    the sea
              -voice
      you sing
          AGAIN!

          LXVI

How do you open the rock?
The key to stone is
where?

(And he went up
over the hill, puzzled
about many things,
              almost dreaming.
There were fledgelings
in the young branches,
flying all around him,
worried, and frightened.
He said to them,
"Never mind, little ones,
I am looking for a way
to unlock stone—
              not to break it."
But they could not answer him.
They were trying to fly
higher.

How do you take
what is a present

with thanks? and without saying
thank you?

(He was not a wise man,
not quite foolish.
He did not like the life
below him;
but he knew so little!
what was ahead.

The wind, now, how
can you tell where it comes from?
really comes?
Not just that which moves
because the other
stirs through it.

(And he came to a place
where the road
was thick with brush.
But he was anxious to go on,
and did.
And the thick brush opened
to a flat place.
He could have thought
that he was the first man there,
but he saw wood,
cut and stacked,
and left there to rot—
old wood—rotten at the ends—
that glowed in the dark,
being damp
                and abandoned.

The key to stone?
(He had almost forgotten that,
—and the last glint of light—
a red patch on an old tree—
made him afraid
-almost afraid-
though he kept on.
Climbing.

Where has the wind gone?
There is no new wind here???

(He came to broad water.
There was still enough light to look,
and he saw two water beetles:
they were arching and contending
on the soft flow.
Were they fighting, or making love?
He wondered about it,
but he knew so little.

The moon, with fire,
or is it a fire*fly*?
Above us the moon.

(He looked out on the land,
and he compared what he saw—
the high land
above the low
                from which he came.
"This land is older than that land.."
He said it without thinking.
Then he thought,
and wondered at what he had said.
He was high
-high enough-
but the peaks were still above him.

Stone, and the stone swings open.

Wind, and the wind moves through.

Fire, and the moon lights up.

(He never came back,
and because he had gone
(before he was forgotten)
men who had laughed
when he was still with them
called him wise.

LXVII

Even in the final grip,
the dance—
            (continuum)
goes on-
            on - on—.
Is it sadness?
(flight of the bird)
no—
        on—on.

Quiet of that going
on -
        no -
what one - no—
on -
        no -
no - on—

no *one*
            every -
goes on.

What is it—
                done?
on.
        The grip on
somewhere - on
the word -
                to return.
no /cross out/
no return—
the dance - the bird
flies
        up—
joy in the lungs,
one last breath—
breathing the last -
on.
Empetrum,
on a rock—
the rock is here.

What to become
                    on
head down
                    singing,
does one sing?
Do I?
          On—
all is on—
not cancelled—
how the hand continues—
it touches on.

To get away from the sun!
It is not breath,
at least it is not
as it might be,
the singing,
face of the morning.
I look out,
but I cannot go.
On.
          Journey on.
pedal note,
how it comes in.
It does cohere,
others
          cohere.
It snatches the hand,
breaks the bones,
brittle,
with this much—
to come back?
I do not.
              On.
The tensions—
spaces between them.
On.
Where? Capstone?
Stone is—
              on.
The breath fractures—
to catch again—

G.M.   Totenfeier,
or Varlaam singing

the wings of the bird
in my hands.
Somewhere to fly up—
stay on—
a bar of light
takes me.
Whatever it is —
to go out—
to come back in
                    again.
There is little of it
in a little time.
The spaces open.

There is sound
far in the back
                    ground—
shining - it makes
something on.
I will not go there,
never reach it,
and the juxtaposition:
So what!
On.
As a man lives,
he goes into his death.
Some cannot.
The pain does not come,
and he laughs
fragile laughter.
The heart constricts for him,
and he labels it
'sentimental' as if
that were a bad word.
Well, let him know,
or let him sleep.
The going on
becomes a task
—or a place-
take your choice,
or as you are chosen.

I sit here,
hardly in the world,
if I ever was,
simply a part,
not without ending
on.
Whoever it is,
someone knocks,
I am not at home.
I cannot see him.
If he will read the note
he may know that I have gone.
A long journey.
It could be
that I will come back
nothing is to be scanted—
nothing left behind.
The dishes are washed—
or not.
(Spot of blood—
                    mine?
The floor comes clean—
that warmth
its relief.

No anger.
            No return.
On -
        joy-on.
Join—.

LXVIII

A man's foot,
which is his own
to use by
force of the flight
upward—
how the foot will leave the ground

as surely as a wing
                feather.
That it is light in places
where lightness is called for,
as the wing may press
heavy,
        or in heavy air.
There is no paradox,
contradiction is not in terms,
only in leaving
what one should not leave.
We have sung out
many times
                -all of us-
in just those silences,
crushed or crowded.
This man feels little more,
or *I* do—
Trying to keep balance,
and the foot measured.
That which might hoild
onto the ground—
that other sustained
as deflection bears it.
when last I knew this—.
That nonesense is coherence.
the foot takes off.

Break and give in the seams.
To heal, walk out,
learn *how* to walk.
The feather catches in the heel.
The man? which of us?
looks forward—
fire tracks behind him.
The losses cut.
Free of them
the step
        ascends.
Pushed forward—light on light—
it opens—
                does not break.
Becomes.

The wisdom—
                    say it so—
a few hours
-brief enough the sleep-
the walk again.
(A time for walking.
Dew washes clear.
I have thought, 'with all this behind me'
that it is not behind—
not the view, that way.
It lies evenly,
distance, but not direction.
The foot touches
                    there.
Take it on—
emerging as the man
who talks.

The child said something:
'dark of blood'
that red is the color of sadness,
as sad is heavy,
so the blood—
the heavy blood held
by the foot.
Its heel trails.

The foot slipped
                    once,
over and out,
direction—
                    in again.
A man walks.
I walk
        slipping.
Sharp stone in the river—
at ford—
and the foot slips.
Lest he dash his foot—.
The blood weeps,
as if for sin—
staunched, or washed away.

A level bar, a shadow
across the road
in early morning.
But the tree is dead,
and the bark scales from it.
Walk by.
Around.
Death in stepping over—
toward the outside.
On.
but no one listens.
The road is lined with dying,
scream is mute,
but it is there.
Many have come—.
—hangs in the air.
A man's foot —
poised.

(All that is not known,
and would be
where the hand slacks off
and we forget.
the foot takes up.
Synthesis but not synthetics.
How to extract
what remains from the light,
put forward
                into the deep of it.
Collection of bones.
Leavening of land.

The foot moves off
as if it were disembodied.
It possesses a part
on its own.
the man above it foreshortens.
His size, or below that,
the bar of shadow
which becomes his—
the tree forgotten
or cut down.
Walking, but with eyes closed,

merely the rhythm.
No ground covered.
The movements are outside
all the same.
Nothing left behind.
We are there
without going,
and the journey
in its length
stands still.
To the sea and from the sea—
the sound of it
-rising-
          blind will see,
deaf follow the tides.
The outer sounds,
across the islands
-far reefs-
               once touched
by step
          taking off.

LXIX

I hear through my eyes—
sound,
          as the sea rises up.
Tide is the seeming
-growth and retreat—
stone against pebble against sand—
awash.
When all is alive,
the senses cross.
Yes, yes the view,
but how do you live with that?
Set me up for a couple of days,
perhaps I can tell you stories,
but I doubt it.

I am hedged in.
Sound will open.
The falls
        down
               there.
I do not see them
-hear as well-
the fading light has caught me.
Falling.

In this place,
these public rooms of others,
it makes no difference.
I had it all to do before.
I am not unhappy
if my eyes would take me straight,
I'd—
but the sound is in.
The sound is always there.
And I, in love,
in love / fiat /
with all I wasted,
nothing more, now.
No surfeit.
Wind and cricket
              see
me through your
              ear / eyes.

It has come to me—
I have never wished a man
to do
what he did not have
in himself—
         his purpose—
without measure.
It would decay within me—
in him.
Leave us then, to our own dreams.
Yet there are those
each day
who ask it :
that we deny ourselves

as they set us up,
believing they have such rights.
and in that right
a power over us,
not to walk out
to the falls.
Stay here, and listen
to their talk.
The senses cannot cross.

(Up the road
the morning following,
in rain and wind,
to the remains of a house
falling in on itself,
but aloof
            and noble—
outside of coercion.
Only the cloud and rain drift.
A few leaves falling.

We walked out,
leaving them to finish
whatever it was
they thought they might—.
Buzz of talk
            receding.

(To put it back—
to put it all back.
I need no following,
though I may like
a certain part of it.
What must I do
to place it in small sayings
when the noise is large?
All these things interlock,
and I'd like a short day
to go for a walk.

Or to think,
following escape.
Madness in seed,
hint of it—

Nathaniel Tarn

what we throw out
at hazzard.
A guess at weather
-time of year-
why do we do it ?
If life is,
          so is death.
Harbinger :
               The cracked seed,
whatever remains at joins.
Walk on that way—
the woods are open.
In the fall
               these spaces.
Whoever sits down
roots in his own place.
How are we set down ?
Ah ! to put it all back.

(In the middle of the night,
A friendly face at the window.
Time to move on.
Passing—
               not the passage
through,
and the lights flaring
against the clouds
lowering over mountains,
not familiar,
but of shapes familiar.
Altars,
and the last rites
held at altars—
some cruel
               -unthinking-
(but that is hardly cruel)
rise in certain lights
to certain mornings.
How one things of it,
even half asleep :
Requiem—
that final opera
for the dead—

not to listen to—
but to be calmed.
The living into that death.
Wherever and whatever
seeming to perform.
We were out once more,
the illness having hold.
No, the poem cannot make itself
without a maker.
I suppose that,
but have no truth of the matter.
We 'made it home.'
After that journey, tried to turn to things
left hanging before—
but somehow couldn't.
They wouldn't do.
It was all so immediate—
such defeat.
In a place where it
did not need to happen!
No matter.
          It did.
The voices of days
cutting through—
but there was nothing to cut.
Impalpable as air—
a malign temper.
Could I reach over it?.
Did they know
          me?
Too much of it.
I remember only the journey,
and that was fair enough.
How a man travels—
simple and ordained
by his sense of time—
riding it.
I gather.
         So,
and morning requiem.

Oh god, for whom no god,
let me, awake,
arise.

LXX

How can I say anything?
except directly?
that address?
(I do?)
Is it heard?
It is the mistake
which orders it.
Canonize what you do not understand.
It is a way of dealing with it.
Ashes make a song.

In case—
as it is that language
of insurance—
something to set by—
wait until the house burns
or the stable door
                    shuts.
I am no stranger
to one cellar hole
set now in the woods,
fields grown up around it,
and a tree
the size of a woman's waist
-larger-
jutting at right angles
between the stones.
In case of
            what?
Where did they go?
Was it slow sinking?
Char and ash?
How long ago?
These questions
fully realized.
And I plant one more tree
inside.
            There,
in case.

(The hands are washed.
Thus saith the lord.)

Scattered,
            the pieces may be
fitted together in a wind.
Passes through.
settles.
Cry of a bird.
(Could be a cat.
It is early.
            Not awake yet.)
What I had earlier—
more than I like to think:
Ashes make a song.
The bone ringed around that.
Heap of bones dropped,
sharp edges—
the spines of burning.
and one more take:
How can I say anything
at all?

The actual events.
We make so much of them!
Never bothering with antecedents
—the set up-
-what came prior.
Little happens there,
and the motto reads:
"Come to where the action is."
Yet, those still places,
interstices of night—
candle or electricity
burning
            on.
The concept/preconcept
happens there.

Showering refigured.
Things will never return to normal—
they never were.
Ah, you pepsi-generation.

Lew Welch

314

Of that great realm,
the possibilities.
sieze on the day.
In a way and manner
speaking.
What makes it relevant:
heaved from the roots—
once
          down again.
A clutch on old things,
this clustering,
Hegel   little learned, and less deduced,
the histories.
His story told in gravesclothes.
Becomes a sadness,
fear in dreams,
perhaps no dream at all.
Make of it another song—
(care in ashes—
                    cerements—
fixed.

"Nothing happens."
Anger in the tone.
"It's all so empty."
As if it might be filled
from desire.
Let it grow—
no push or pull.
Where are the mistakes?
I heard it plain,
all of it from one source,
datum,
          and it does not change.
Broken stem—
a fingerlength burning.
The straw twists
as heat draws in.

Eventually
          you walk against yourself—
meet one man
          coming back,

or sounds between the echoes.
The sme man?
However they are found:
the interstices—
windows opening—
glass colored.
Poised at seasons
to catch light or tone,
shade of a meaning
caught.
Before such a fact,
the edge on which to split
the echo.
It is there that saying
becomes words,
words symbols.
What is behind them
holds cause.
Cause remains.
Events fan out—
away—.
It is darkness,
it is fortune.
It is little,
and little more.
A way,
          and each
is tried.
Put these together.
We will talk.

LXXI

I do, on rising,
greet myself
as much in sadness
as in joy,
          no more.

Old pleasures gone,
the new ones come.
I see this light,
no older than a day before,
though measured.
And I may be,
                both.
I'll not take it lightly.
Rising is the first chance—
a risk.
I do not feel the heat or cold
until later.
                (much later)
One thing at a time.
The senses do agree—
find themselves,
but slowly, gently.
The shadow passes.
The sun lends an eye,
or cloud its silence.
Here again,
                not here,
the reaches in—
passages out.
Downstairs without thinking it.
So little to go on.

(It all started to move once more—
the heavy rains more general,
but the colors that year
stayed on.
                The year seemed gentle,
though certain things suffered.)

I miss certain things—
those that I laid by last night—
nothing here.
Well, go outside.
Walk a few minutes.
It will come clear.
Mislaying some of it,
the rest may come to light.
Weak as the motion,

it comes stronger—
water reaching
near and far shores
at the same moment.
Come back in.
'Righted round'
good vernacular for it.
Cup of tea.
Whatever was left from last night.
Out once more.
It is stronger.
"It" or myself?
Is there a difference?
Could anyone tell?

Motion—
            down—
whatever beat
the tread beat here before.
Deja vu—
scuffing the leaves
any season.
Resonance changes—
returns—
            brittle through wilt.

But it is a day to think of journeys.
Is it true?
            I leave today?
not tomorrow?
I am not ready—
but that fear,
an old one,
familiar,
comes from inexperience.
Ready or not.
Go.
So much to put here—
to put there,
so they balance.
Can they? balance?
or revert?
An old man struggling

with baggage in way stations.
Clearly not up to it.
Go.

(And a few words
before leaving
           came in
God knows how or where:
"Where or whatever
they said of it
sounded like rain
on old tin—
perhaps a shed roof."

Did it say the right things?
There is nowhere,
as this place is nowhere.
Going cannot touch it.
What did the mountain sing?

Lew Welch   "This is the last place. There is nowhere else to go."
That simple, but we don't believe it.
Go.
Eventually we find out.
It is not that hard in the going.
As there is no there,
that hangs us
on the edge of a cliff
by the teeth.
Nothing very wise either way.
The locus?
Don't give it that way—
simple, but not fee simple.
The world!
and it's not a cosmos,
macro or micro—
just what I can see of it.
Now, later,
in moonlight filtered
through the last of the rain
clouds that don't move much,
though they have no further power.
Another sun will fix them.
They can only hang

until the fire hangs them.
It comes on quickly,
far too quickly.
I am guilty of too much,
and it is too little—
neat, to hang it up that way.
(All the while,
an old man struggling with baggage,
who shouldn't be here.
Once I said something:
that what moves least moves most—
but that was music.
Interval to interval
                    spaced.
Isn't this?
Strange sort of music,
but I hear it.
Setting a bonfire
where there was already a fire—
sharper
          clear blue flame.
Not redundant—
bringing fire to fire—
the ice or snow to water,
melted as a principle.
Rising—
tides of rising.
Ritual required.
And yet there is no place.
None for it,
words rushing and tumbling
out of the endless forests.
Floods have been,
will be again—
and in the morning,
this high greeting
to myself,
and to those others
with me,
shadows in the dust—
a dust I make:
What I have been,

and where I have—
endless float—
the comet's tail.
There was no wisdom.
Could not be.
Rising in the morning,
what is left to greet?
The mirror opens—
as myself,
will catch the light.

LXXII

Where the leaf lay,
a figure in the sand,
wet from the rain
and the flagging year,
it pressed itself
and was gone.
I looked at it,
wondering where I might see
as much again.

Level, or below the level,
where the root first stretches, it
continues to stretch,
no matter where the mountains are.
The highest branch
is nothing, if the lowest root
contiguous, has failed.
And both will fail
without the leaf.
The fruit is fragile,
but it holds a life.

I had half a mind
-no matter what I had-
I filled myself with motion
from that moment on.

A leaf in concept,
or a leaf so central,
the veins had sweat
into the rock—
their stains as permanent.

(And all around
                    the trails of
other lives
            as certain
in their will to die—
or so to live it through.

Sweet, to quicken
                    and to fall.

To avail myself—
to find that place
where everything is spaced
in such economy
that no thing extra
cumbers—
                    no clutter
and no waste.
But that is talking
as the machine talks—
and wealth is not in it.
Delight here—
in this which is overfull,
or there, in deserts,
where the sparseness
seems
and gives away
its amplitude.

That's it!
I cried in excitement—
almost as if I were drunk.
Running up the beach
in the cool sting
of sand and spray
from a south swell
-the breakers-

I had found the ranger
knew his commentaries
would unlock
the natural.
(And the others ?
are they any less ?
natural ?)
It is here I found
the print of the leaf—
his story.
All the genders one,
as, all the stories.

Face in the crowd
which became
more than a face.
And where she sat
next to me—
fingers touched
tentatively—
so warm!
Finally the eyes turned,
questionning and full.
Limpid *is* the best word,
no mater if it's overused.
A shy smile,
first from her,
and then from me.
No questions,
and nothing further.
Print of the leaf.
Time to move on.
His story.

But illness takes a toll.
What is not old,
becomes it.
I am sitting
on the edge—
still rising—
the root ?
the leaf ?

Aleator—the gambler—
in his last game.

Bent to the work,
it is only the work that counts.
In the words of work,
only the words get done,
and there is a space
left over.
I tried to bridge the two.
No, it is too late
to turn back.
It was always too late
to make the work count.
It comments.
At best, it moves through
his story, braided
with the fixtures.

Another winter,
and I am not ready for it.
In no sense.
But it comes,
following the print of the leaf.
And if it freezes now,
the print will remain
until the snow has gone once more.

Looking at most people—
most seed—
it is difficult to imagine them
coupled, fucking.
Yet the young are around us—
they do.
Daily these reflections.
Something moves,
leaves the print of passing
or rising:
a sign.
It seems faster than it did.
Regret, as age advances.
The years spill into each other,
and I look for the print,
care that it does not blur.

Fixed on that,
I think it will burn clear—
the sun.
And that design
behind the sun.
(Perhaps the leaf's print.)

Urging and urging,
and nothing comes of it.
Is there a joy like this?

Finding what has been composed?
The use in it?
How to create
· from what was created—
then its use—
to free the forms in stones
or wood or leaves,
or metals in the earth
-the gaseous metals-
Such as these take off.
There is the life
of fossils - track and raindrop
fixed in stone—
a sedimentary rock
that froze in air.
The tempera, ours,
and heavy on our shoulders—
pressing down.
A place to sing in joy.
To take the way
as found.
I *am* found
by the poem,
by the leaf,
the print of leaf
the outlines of a star,
out
    in the rising of the day.
Hold, as hold on.
(Once held, the power's lost.)
And we'll not come again
unless—
whatever of us

(teeth are the hardest)
keep.
That one does not think
always of these things,
keeps in mind
the tracks
where things have been:
Next/ the leaf
a diagram drawn with a stick
a child's doing
-something- the oldest.
Track of a slug
shining—dried before water.
It was to this place
I came.
Where I stayed.

LXXIII

As the process,
which I had in hand once more,
I turned it over.
In the turning, found it ran
like quicksilver, balls and pools of it,
through my fingers,
coherent, yet breaking
free as formed.
Different in this from sand or dust.
It delighted me,
and I went on with it.

There are those who say
of the search for clarity,
or delight in it
                    once found,
that it is trivial.
Let them.
            Some of them are good people,

but in this,
          thank god,
they are wrong.
That: there are many ways
to look for it.
That: it is elusive, or difficult,
often abused as word or concept,
I cannot deny.
And yet it is there—
a prism
        clear
in every facet—
where and wherein the light strikes.
Say when!
It is just now coming clear to me,
how important that is,
and how it will stand up
to any abuse.
Clarity is the giant among us.
Its force will not be denied for long.
We return to it—
to that greatness.
We knew it when we were young,
turned away,
and then came back,
older men,
        not wiser,
but with much burned out
that needed to go.
And that simplicity
is no longer simple.
It weaves a rich texture
of many threads.
Buried sound—
the clock complaining of time
deep in its works.
(If I work in a hurry,
do I work *against* time?)
Posing the question,
its final loss.)
I've spent a deal of it,
find certain points coming thin

in myself—
the bones show through,
but the process continues.
The concept overriding,
and the particulars.
A medical theorem.
We do not move
without both of them.
I cannot write for the lines.
It is less than dutiful,
work for the caitiff.
How can a man
put himself on that line?
I remember as a child,
the game.
It started:
Ash a tac nein viels?
Scrambling the letters and the parts.
(I don't know how many lives
a cat may have.
I love my cat.)
The game goes on.
There is no way to stop it.
It would be easy
to think death the croupier.
I'm not so certain.
The pure product,
but we had better stay
with the process—
route.

We are asked a number of questions.
It is wrong to answer,
or to try to answer them.
Man working?
need no signs of it.
He works,
and the work gets done.
It is easier,
more pleasant in belief,
but it gets done
even in void—
a mathematical black hole.

These places—
                    the coal sack—
spaces between galaxies.

In speaking of process,
we often do the work.

The weight of it—
would we wish that
on anyone ?
Try to go another way,
but keep to the one
that lies to the feet.
It will sustain.
Sharp stones take a man on.
Rising upon—
                    an elation.
The vine swings from the trees,
holds them together.
Climb, if you must.

And,
        fear each doubling
of the sound,
                    take in
the note,
or let it go,
                    loosed.
It will hold.
These
        are the morals.
Rest go hang.

Nor what pleases on the page.
If it does,
take up with it.
Even the ear
or hand
can play it false.
It is the right of it
to be.
In that right
much felicity.

Process is union.
A man's life.
I'll lay it on the line
once more—
not that
it will mean that much
to anyone but myself,
but that it is the work.
The shaman heals,
but not himself.

There is a time
to tell stories,
and another to hold off
in medias res.
Tell how the story is—
not told,
but something,
as cartographer.
The whole map,
source and delta—
far at sea.

It dims.
Even if I could travel
through constellations
light years apart,
if I kept on travelling,
some light would blur,
and some of them fade
out.
It is not consistent
to hold on
where one no longer is.
Flowing in the sea,
a man reaches
for the gong buoy,
but his arm will dislocate,
pull off,
if he insists
that it stay there.
He, putting off to sea

(in rout of phosphorous
the long way—
voyage.
We have to give up
many things. It is
simply distance.
If it comes too hard:
This was good.
That will be.
The bell on the gong—
far to the east'ard—
sounds on.

Shippensburg, Pa. Rain again,
the same spot in the morning.
Will it clear?
as it did yesterday?
later?
Forms one unity.
Might, another.

What is set down
must be needed—
ration for the journeying—
a long way off or on.
Nothing else is needed.
Grant you pleasure
in the route.

LXXIV

Right at it!
to deal with the fact—
not talk about it,
Simplest words—
the facts:
"Ted's in bare feet,
and he ate breakfast—
bare feet."

Well, I like air around my body.
It is hard to think
that others enclose
at the places
where I must open.
but this is the fact—
only myself
confessing.
                    Confusing,
not pejorative.
But when the little girl
is surprised at me
-the barefoot man-
she shows where she is,
posits me
at another place.
It is good that this happens.
Too much politeness
in the world.
I woke up this morning,
and I was glad.
It took a long time
to reach this:
To know what is long—
what cuts off—
the brittle grasses
broken in the snow—
web and cobweb,
green of the fragile spring
coming through them.
It is inverted each year.
So old / so new.
Don't try against that.
Sometimes I am forced
into the work—
nothing else that can be done.
I *need* to work.
Thirsty, and the end
gives water.
All day,
all my days,
windburn on the cheeks.

Lost loves,
loves to be,
silence,
                except for slight wind—
the head of the draw.
I think I move
with these things
(tentative)
their silence,
beyond what I may make,
though the making
keeps me alive
in them.

The study?
The place where it is done?
Everywhere .

H.C.
Notch Brook, 9/16/75
(I was sitting with a friend
among enemies.
The hawks clustered.
Their concerns were immediate.
They had no ideas.
From the ground,
it was good to look up.

He recedes into the far air,
but he has been here.

It is so easy to pick up
from the air around.
Hard to put it back
where it came from.
That is the work—
sometimes sustained on very little.
It is arduous,
with ardours
                compressed
into the place
where.
There must be
flame and flare
around it.

My aura—
from a hand or foot—
free to the air.
Take off—
a free impingement.

At times (from what it makes—
how it centers
too exactly—
a life not made.
The harshness
of an outer desert.
Must take that risk.
The resources are our own.
There is no way to go beyond,
without them :
                        Inner,
how that sounds.
The echo or reverberation,
so that we forget the fact.
Enough to let it be—
(shed carapace
that it grows another.)
Dig of the nail
into the side of a rock
holding to anything
that the climate willed
as a vehicle.
Carries weight.
Color of chameleon—
that change,
but it takes time,
and there is the moment before—
to be found out—
predator at the pounce.
Escape is possible.
Not always the wise course, though.
In fright and anguish,
we *reach* hold,
and then go on.
However we decide,
we are moved,
not moving.

Conduct and conductus—
the ease /
          mesh /
take it in.
Or the other—
mass ordinary
to the day.
I'd sensed the pride
in exact strokes—
once received
at the source—
the news there.
It is the wind following—
hardly beginning.

LXXV

"The power flows through me."
a word of terror,
                    or of hope.
Off side of the coin.
Where ? that other world ?
The man is speaking to me.
Is it his voice ?
Do I hear him,
                    even now ?
The days have shifted,
but we did not leave
                    each other.
What he said, remains . .
(Slight insistence, and I
hear it—
          chrrr of a squirrel
scolding.
          What is he scolding ?
No one there,
                    no other
squirrel.

                    It is
for the world to hear—
no more
            no less.
I am alone or not alone—
no matter.
The power stays in.
Stays on.
I hear—but why?
What is it to hear?
Not to hold on—
the power flowing—
never stopped—
whirled and siezed—
its own objects,
using them as its own—
losing / loosing.
(And the only thing to find
now—
            a scrap of paper—
that man's address,
as if—
            but no, not his.
Another's,
            as it wills.
Is it will?
Power from another source—
from such an
                    other.
Do we find it?
Do I?
Who are you?

The man comes towards me
-straight on-
his mark at my throat,
so I fear it—
And one dead man,
spoke of the others
who sharpened blades
by turning them—
that fine a balance.

A. Peterson

At the Back of the
North Wind

It was here I spoke
out of a dream—
and that dream
eddying with the power
which lies before the knife edge,
behind it—
                is it only
as a wind passing through.
That place behind—
of calm and ice—
the silences of those forewarned.

Threads tightened—
web or mesh—
and how they're worn
is as the wearer moves
on or through—

Scrap, song, or spill—
lay out
            play out—
the words mean nothing,
exactly as they fill the space
or move in space—
the power gone along.
Stream bank caves—
silt and salt
collapsing
to the sea.
That outward place—
a man upstairs,
and late again.
Well, he hardly knew,
but all his voice
was lost—
far, far over in the sea.

(Do not look in the source,
an eye there
winks out.
It will not find
its forture—
                "The power
flows through me,"

337

and little choice
for power or its instrument.

Gently, the warmth dissolves.
The face goes limp.
(Losing one,
                    I saw that
misapprehended—
hardly knew it,
mistook the power stirring it,
leaving it
                    untouched.)

It goes by the board,
whatever 'it' is.
And we are out and outward,
looking for what we never had—.
Flows through.
No one knows,
                    and no one—
(sound of the waters,
late at night.
They rise,
                    their certain plunge
in a dream
flows through—
and land and wind,
and life
            and ice
and death.

The sign is water,
going through it—
that haste,
or brittle?—
left for flow—
rivers—endlessly—
on the way to—?
I can't answer that,
nor may it be
                    answered.
Life or love of it.
I see the man again,

sitting at his table,
simply and quietly,
The power
        as the power
may.
    I do not know.
It touches me.
It touches all of us.
Some time we may find it,
but hardly now.
as the storms may come
and blind us
        temporarily—
we are caught.
Held, but not in firmness.
The power, always the power,
flowing through.

LXXVI

Dust.
Grey.
A pinch of dust.
These stones.
And, clear,
a hill
    rising from November.
There is wind
eddying,
skirl and twist,
a tension /
      / edge /
scream at the turn,
moan
    in the corner.
Sigh.
    Such heaviness,
waiting for snow.

All Hallows,
        All Saints,
The Day of the Dead.
As,
   in that darkness,
wait
    for prayer.
A way out.
It catches,
       as the luck
runs out.
A year of darkness,
if the prayer,
        unanswered,
fails.
Plumbs the depths—
sounds
    leaden
pearls.

Stippled back,
or heaved as mud—
dull—
    river runs in rain.

Tales of ghosts,
of whom ghosts are—
their being.
Who am I ? The ghost
preceding them—
I rise.
    Go down.

(All that is best
lies burning
      solid
under ashes—
       burned out.
Shadow on the fire
once lit for warming—
warmth. Its latter course
shut up.
    It loses.

Falls away.
The singer faints,
The dancer sleeps.

And frost that hung on trees
all day.
            It would not go—
the sun, a pale reflection,
cold,
            and in the cold.
The moon would do as well.
High haunts.
The cry of wolves,
and sounds caved in.
The dark of iron,
lightened.
            Grey.
A little life inside it.

Then
to see what the morning wills of me.
Not in saying,
                  feeling, perhaps,
where feeling ends
nerve against nerve—
the will—
            an air—
these mornings—
                  will—
and will the air.

Yet nothing no longer here
holds it.
the grip will not let go,
nor does it suffice.
How often?
Who stands in the dust?
bit of old bone
            or tooth?
I come closer - yet -
and where.
The bloom in the stone—
a year's curse
to cast it . .

Out of the head, and singing,
pass not the day,
or pass again.
Feed on that.
Make sense of it.
Of whom?
Hardly a voice
yet formed—
a structure, broken.

They rose early
and went out
looking.
A precision
overlooking the hills—
the far mountains and the sea.
The old men walk again.
They beg a pardon
as they close on flesh:
We are forbidden,
cannot recognize
the ghost
from where we are.
We must.
Pay lip service and go on.
An ill wind
stays above ground—
foundering below
to drag men under.
Take this toll—
a candle or a flower.
Open the wound,
and as the wound is coffin,
seal it.
Down among—
ah - darkness -
where a world
that was and is
and never was
                    waits.
Dying. In dying days of year,
the night.

LXXVII

Verging on the fun of the thing,
it will be:
Where a man starts off
in the cold of the early morning,
carrying a light with him.
It will be,
if his sense of being
includes play,
that he does not feel himself
bound to a working,
or return from it.
That he will work in play,
wonder that he grows tired,
takes a nap at midday
on a full stomach.
Others set off with him,
but they walk in fear,
and the darkness is oppressive.
(They must see to work—
danger of a hand cut off—
an eye blinded.)
They do not see the light
striking the branches,
or the early shadows
on the sun.
They cast up accounts,
and reckon what the week was 'worth.'
They are frightened:
He has started to sing.
The sound of their machines
cannot drown it—
high, soaring like a bird,
hovers,
        planes on the air—
a hawk's wing—
feather catching the sun—
pure joy of it—
his song.

He will not stay long with them,
and after he has gone

the others will laugh,
call him crazy—
forgetting their fear,
or whistling into the wind
against it.

(The low wind,
trail of exhaust.
And they go home
to curl up in the ashes.
Asleep. Dead in their sleep.
Outside, he is still walking,
singing.
For joy of the moon now—
white night in winter.
He has forgotten them.
They never knew him.
Ludens / Ludens.
Ha!

The urge itself
makes work easy—
not to be forced.
To forget the whip's end,
or an anonymous bolt.
(Even now - alone -
at my own work -
I hear sounds.
Those who make them
'get around early in the morning
to get something done.'
They go home with nothing.
The substance leaks
and loses—
blood on a frozen road.
I cannot forget or forgive that.
To be born into it
is not to complete it:
Not as a cipher.
The man is still singing.
I hear him
-far off- the sea
in a shell.

Rush of the blood.
the ear and tide
which coexist.
Warm, and drowsing
by a new fire.

(The man will not ask
to come in.
Often, not sure that he wants to.
If he is asked,
he may. Don't count on it,
nor on him.
He flows as quicksilver
flows—
coalesces
   in new forms
-asunder-
    but himself.
He brings together
as he will.
Skylarking down the wind,
or through the rain.
In frost or hail,
his voice and song.
The others, dumb and spent
in sleep they do not understand,
as waking, they cannot.

Times come as holidays.
The work closes,
ends broken.
But he is still at it—
and finds no need—
impatient at the break
the others live for.
'When men still planted elms—'
the line occurs to him.
It was then they lived
closer to the household gods.
And what they did
brought singing, often,
-unbidden-
water in pure wells.

fouled now—
a rusty tap
                leaking.

He runs away,
and despises himself
for hiding.
It cannot be hidden.
nor found in hiding.
He is lonely for his kind,
despite the song,
(the sting proclaiming it.)
But he cannot go back.

Karl Kraus

Of two evils
he must choose neither one.
Can he stop?
or is he tempted?
(The dark side.
A face he cannot show,
although he would.
He might, by starlight,
take that chance.
Or in reflection.

And in the morning,
those who pray for the shadows
will return..
Those who do not,
travelling in the hot sun,
will find the shadow gone—
the leaves tilted on edge—
the rocks, merciless—
the waters burning—
salt for many wounds.
The man is singing,
but the man is gone.
His song from the headlands,
islands,
                knolls of fir and cedar.
If the song is heard at all,
it comes as bright pain—
knife
                cutting

cobweb broken
down / dooms / death—
but not quite.
It is blunted,
wondering,
until another comes.
Leans into the wind,
and learns his song.

LXXVIII

If it make—
(If I make it)
the tense-improbable—
tenses of their habit,
form of being,
past or any other,
all imperatives
stopped—
            shock still.
Other tenses
            weed growth
out of mold
-swamp-sluggish-
getting on.
Finding the impurities.
It will break
as the switch,
endlessly back and forth.
The enginery:
make and break—
the two synonymous.
As the death implies:
It breaks,
            or if.

Taking it over,
here is what was lost.

Under the snow all winter,
it stayed put.
The clutter, obliterated,
is still there.
Nothing loses
unless to dull stain—
a rust that will not rub out.
Other stains,
but none so grievous—
showing
        the wound.
Wound that makes
more wound,
spreads itself—
a fever made of dreaming—
madness—if it make.
And skills at making,
where there is no sense of it.
Aimless,
        to be doing.
Those who cannot stop
                      are
once on the road
from which there is no turning.
Back is easier,
but the barriers contain wandering.
a few shards—
these still lying under snow.
Keep the old flints.
They make new fires.
Fires burn well—
hot—and new from them.
(Shovel the ashes—
let them sink in snow.

Some of us were here first,
and will not let it escape
fact
    or what was made
as fact.
Let it be known:
              We stay.

A firmness without anger.
The barricade is there,
if need be.
Take it as the sound
from a depth—
a distance
               heralded
(low voice)
Trumpet and drums.
It made.

Outside, a storm.
But is it weather?
Or is it made of what we
think about the weather?
Take these questions
as the artifacts—
not the answers.
The easy way, scanting.
A privilege after the fact.
This is the way to draw on.
Of this,
          his story.
No one will return,
but no one came.
(We were here to stay.)
It is hard to say this—
to grasp *what* it is
that makes the saying..
But it is there,
and it is the only sanity.
Days spent at it.
Give over the thinking!
This is the way
to that road which contains.
Blinders
          and a full trough of oats.
Lean going:
A sack and a bedroll—
a sharp knife.
Maps, or a clear idea.
That's best—
an empty head—

a wise one.
Step over the fence,
and the forest waits.
a path
     and suddenly the sea.
Good to walk there,
shuffling the sand,
as sand is not static.
Exemplar of living:
Someone to talk to!
How much that is needed,
and yet denied.
Talk—words—
but the senses clash,
and an incredulous smile
If it make.
No refrain.
It takes up from its movement.
(And he sings this song:)
        Echo
            only
        by what
        is worthy
        sometime
                 sound
        its weight.
Search for sound.
Star shine first,
but clear.
The snow blurs,
cannot make.
That softness.
Revolves upon itself,
returns a spectrum.
A hint as caution.
No one on that side
of it.
Against a going—further—
to further it.
Made.

LXXIX

The fire is up!
Leisurely.
Then snap of the wood—
frost and split.
the time is ripe for it—
scream of the woods
in winter.
An agony,
                but not a dying.
Agony reverses sleep.
and keeps in motion.
Blood for the pounding,
road on road
the wilderness:
Bewilder/ness.
(Standing to sniff the air,
fox on the prowl,
scent of game.

Night again,
and all that chills it
stands   .   in   .   close   .
a day returned,
                silent.
slow heartbeat
                muffled
hammering—.
Lace—
        uptilted
shield of the snow
catches in rising sunlight.
I am abroad to it.
Walking the high spaces—
pure air around me.

And as the ice melts
it comes closer
full circle
to a night of freezing.
Fire is up,
and well may it be—

releasing the light of many summers
in small compass—
tropic air.

Take season by the season's stride.
Its will my will—
a caution, picking up
a certain path
in all weathers—
vein that leads to heart,
warm beneath,
and then above . .
All that waits
waits bidden.
Accidents do not occur.
The casualty is written in.
(Another log to keep the fire up.)

A theory of return,
but not in theory.
As the world stops?
A candor in that.
It will not.
I came in this morning.
Was I once outside?
It seemed to me I was,
thinking.
Here and here,
I may not have moved—
sucking on the last bone—
emptiness.
I was there, once—
no, here.
I am alone—
this crowd around me?
a lynch mob perhaps.
Alone.
          I say it.
The response is with me,
and then I did
only I thought I did,
or neither.
Tried to open up—

lost the key
somewhere along the roads—.
Aghh!
    The fire needs more wood,
and I need to be elsewhere.

Wind catching my corners,
again a keening sound—
something down over the hills—
drawn down
like a cap to hold
-eye to eye-
and which one
holds the ice?

The Snow Queen   the last splinter of glass?
I'd felt it
festering—a wound
deeper than the others,
lasting into the high time.
To melt,
but not to heal.

And as I was, I felt
my own breath
come back to me—
a nourishment.
It was told me
to say these things—
not what I had thought,
or heard others say—
not the theory—
never a return.
Another log for the fire!

(Anything that touches
congeals—
catches on my windows—
hard to see
the day beyond
-darkening- losing its perspective.
I am a spark
set in the night
that I may not waver,
or go out.

And as I looked into the fire
the last coal fell.
Reached the bottom
stone cold.

However any of this
is set down,
it is set here to rise,
and to rise
                to come new.
The words are the same,
and the fire.
The theory comes later,
or the theory
                not at all.
It is the lock on the door
It is stiff,
and it is rusted—
frozen shut.
But the door will open.
The key is lost—
but behind the lock
a fire is burning.
Attention to the lock.
Pick it!

LXXX

Hard to read in the wind,
when the stars say it,
it is hard.
To listen is harder.
There is space, though,
and in that space, the act:
His Story.
Or how the reading fixes,
as the water holds reflection.
Only the light is fixed—
water always gone—

the movement in the fix,
and there's the reading of it.
I go out to touch,
and only the touch is real.
Empty.
            Yes, and that, too—
the illusion, not the fact.
Leave me the spaces—
islands—
take the solid for its own
dwindling return.
Hard to read,
                    but possibly a reading.
The light outside
lights inside,
leaves the out alone.
Bright stands still in space,
refracts against the shell.
I stand.
            You stand.
We all stand.
The wind flows on.
(Coal sack among the stars.)
Moved closer to it—
standing by the blaze
to warm my hands.
Hard to extract:
Heat from fuel,
truth from marrow—
moments are the only measure.
Reading or firing,
sense along the skin,
and my spark goes out,
cupped in a hand
to shield it from the wind.
Best to face into it.
There are few lessons—
much to unravel,
a tangle of learning
thrown overboard,
snarled in the kelp,
fouled with torn fish gear

brought in—
windrows at tide mark,
left to bed in the sand.
Kick through it, if you like—
fleas for the pains.
Feared to go down again—
that misreading.
Wondering in words.
Caught behind a net
in the stars,
or in the net
                    beyond.
Stars at their breaking point.
Let them talk to me.
Few have,
misreading,
and the wind stands still.

(A governance of things—
that one is set over many.
It was a thought—
found out.
Died before its time,
followed greed—
swallowed—a green fly
and a frog on a hot day.
Whatever mentioned,
it came up for a misreading—
that was the catalyst—
what was realized
                    as needed.
Made: His Story,
through the mistakes—
holes in the mesh
to let the wind
                    through
or free.

A hole in the wall,
or the rock.
Entrance for the sun
as

Tularosa Basin   Puerto del Sol,

raising the words :
open to them.
We are moving inward again.
Granite strike on the teeth—
how one feels about this—
well, his own affair.
I am going elsewhere,
spending thus
                            an afternoon
relaxed against the snowfields
-warmer though-
as if a bear might wake.
Still, the voice in the wind
barely heard.
The written test
a codex
not yet open.
Take care of it.
I am moving once more,
out, to find
a place to stand on—
point of gravitation
whirling.
Space as silent, still.
Breaking a fortune
out of stone
into stone.
Interstices—the lines—
or the sure return.
Eels that spawn in seaweed,
unerring
to a Sargasso, holding sense.
That space, enough.
The mumbled stricture,
and I am left—
caught with the wind.

Trying out of that
to make a substance—
what coheres.
That is the fortune
had in it,
and yet hard to return.

Shadows longer,
the late afternoon,
closer in winter.
Blue shadows,
snow caves, opening,
runnel from below
eating the substance,
read aright.

And they all returned to me.
They had no credence
in the things I had,
and they thought they heard the message
in the earth—
read on the wind.
It was hard to come by.
Hard to feel it.
Well, the sadness answers me.
Read the wind—
once, slowly.
                    Capped
down the sun's
                    set answering.

LXXXI

Temple Stream
1/28/76

A river in new traces
cannot forget its old bed—
returns,
            however briefly,
in flood time—
                    subsides
regretfully,
            quiets once more
under the trees and grasses
bent towards it.
Gnawed in the roots,
these water spirits,
                    and

ready to tear loose,
unerring, to the tide.
And yet they seek the water,
will live nowhere else
save in that delicate balance
where all is a gamble—
where there may be no tomorrow—
the face of the land
                    changed,
the unfamiliar as the usual—
change becomes guardian.
It is always there.
A man follows,
                if he is wise,
but builds higher up—
watching,
            always watching.

Ill water that brings no good,
no bounty
                -fuel or ice-
ill water /
            / still water—
miasma.
(Back eddy—
                whirl of chips—
leaves / foam.
Blue ice
            steadying.
Channel shored.)

Whatever is forgotten
turns over
                upbellied—
fish under the ice—
moves away,
torn from its base.
Churned / ground.
                    (Flour sand :
gold settles.
The heaviness,
still of the air cut through,
even the fish beds scouted.

Surety is in movement,
nothing more.
His story left in rock grooves—
a new white scratch this year.
(Loath to remove,
oh let the sun arise—
in moonset refract this light
that the waters do go down—
the sea accept them
without question,
                    whence or where:
what broke under flow,
or stands—
            a monument.)

Thrust and hammer stroke—
the day alive again—
wind jostle.
The battle of heat
against cold—
                or is it cold?
A moving through,
as simple as that might be.
In one spot of sunshine,
out of the wind,
a waking bird—
its spring song against
a winter silence.
Contra punctum.
Come in—this chill like smoke
hangs in the eaves.
Thrust again—
look for those spaces
wherever they may be
reasons die out
ground.
            stone on stone.
Tentative, a block of sense
blocking it—
spaces clouded over.
Smoke on!

This,
      that is tenacious,
and will not be released—
from us—to us.
The stream takes no notice.
More:
      Nor do forces
which impell.
Curse, as might Ixion—
let him go.
Ajax—ha!
This bravery—nothing—
and the rabbits sleep well
in warm warrens.
The days increase,
but we do not.
Blind heritage—
not even the smoke of a thought.

To tell anything,
becomes an enormity—
forget it—
      as you are forgotten.
Almost to give it up,
but not its edge.
To walk away from it—
yes, but then turn back—
almost—
      not quite—
a foreboding,
      as of a day
2/6/76   that happens
as if nothing had—
a sense of evil—
some calamity—
dull pain
      here,
which will not work out,
but stays
      stuck.
There is the secret:
how to hold the braid,
a number of channels

all entering at once.
And as the stream flows out,
it flows in.
It is tantamount.
What stays in the mind
treats of it,
as the mind entreats.
We are held there.
No passage across this stream
in flood time.
Believe my stricture.
Come back.
A final answer?
A slap in the face—
cold water—
wind later.

How it happens:
Fine seethe—
seethe
        as slide
the long side
lopside
        shadow
down—
        blue cold
snow is
        called
final.
How that much is argued.
Where I go from there.

I remember, years ago,
sitting with him,
talking at random
on an early winter afternoon,
below the farmhouse—
clouds driving from the west,
and I wondered if it meant snow.
Nothing.
They vanished.
As the cloudless sky this morning—
insistent pondering

in the deep sounds,
brushing away from the trance.
The rivers are open,
and the cold deepens.
There is no balance—
balanced, still,
the old and the new
traces.

LXXXII

Wolf moon, and hunger moon,
sickle cold,
a sharp brightness.
Curve of the snow
no longer soft.
Feet draw blood,
and the ice burns red.
A stiff eruption—
                    frost
on the window pane,
traced as if it came
out of a vase.
But still, so still
these many days—
chill factoring
            cold moons
the ravened ones.
Tightened belt against the pain,
and no food for it—
nothing sates.
The sun, an illness under clouds,
the muffling sadness,
ominous—a dread—
nothing to set it by.
Compass spins
            off course.
Raw to the bone—

sinews sow—the white teeth
in a grin—held
spring capturing through green ice,
the eyes open
but unseeing.

Complaint that drifts
smoke to the stars—
a draft which rises
-cold nights- -vapor-
taking light.
The heat becomes thin echo,
paves the zenith,
and the howl of dogs
a ghost of wolves long gone.
"Ah, long ago,

            ago—
is now!

        Ah well!
Ahhh!"
Sinks out—the last coal
dropping through the grate,
and go abroad
at peril.
Magic in the wand—
witch hazel at full moon—
the bark that catches glint,
or holds a frost—
its own as bitter as the night.
Nothing stirs—
the river penned.
Stay clear—
a skate on ice,
scream, and a biting
to the bone again,
where nothing bleeds.

(Somewhere connections
endlessly ringing
tone after tone—
shattering of glass—
scatter on the snow—
murderous shards.

Light so light,
                the heat gone in,
an inward light,
and at the back of light.

Rising into that fullness—
the shadow at noon
blue as gun metal
breaks against another.
It is *all* shadow—
nothing is real.
Lost - lost again.
It might as well be night.
Relief when it comes.
I walk cautiously,
looking for a trail—
lost in its muffling.

(Icicles hung
too long in the wind,
so many snag teeth—
fangs that break—
daggers that give way
to dull pain.
And it goes on—.

Waking,
        I know what I do not
ten minutes after waking.
The connections break,
and I am returned—
ringing in my ears
fainter and fainter—
still as the ice.
Here and now—
the time of the bitter moons.
What I had thought I had,
I lose.
The day is acid.
A dry mouth draws in.
I see so little—
and yet—
                yet, what?

It is this immediacy
into which I wake—
but not yet—
                    not just yet.
Figure of a man
on the hill,
but only his figure,
there is no man there.
Sky paved,
and in the clot,
a final point of light—
day or evening star.
I am reached by it,
and yet—
                    yet not at all.

These echoes in the morning.
Intricate hammers
sounding out of night—
further and further off
the stroke.
They'd have me—
have it.
What is it?
Who can tell me?
Where are you?

Glance-shadow.
and the road stretches
its fingers.
(How I know
where I am not.)
(Here.
in this corner by the chimney,
like a cat
curled in its dream.)
A stare
              not fixed.
No thing fixed.
We think them so,
and then forget
all that was given in the dream—
night gone to another place.

We were there,
but not longer.
Deja-vu? only the night,
and another part forgotten.
Some have called its form madness,
and run from it
or burned it—
destroying only the mirror.
Others say wisdom,
and approach no nearer.
In the low ebb of the year
-the dead season-
it walks more surely,
holds in these shadows—
these moons—
all darkness—mute sound.

Carry some of it
to other times—
a hot coal to lay
among dry twigs.
The days lengthen—
tighten the design.
Then,
        the first thaw—
a sign of flowing water.

LXXXIII

Writing it out:
Commentarium.
What was used?
or lost conveniently?
Ulterior, or faulty memory?
Everywhere the verdigris—
that cover up—
slick as ice or glass.
Hard to recover,

and if it is,
                    what remains?
It is hard to give up
what we have not had,
but think we have.
One way to bridge monotony,
or to keep on going—
wannigan for a long journey.

The cases:
Specie as wampum—
not a primitive exchange
until the white traders thought of it.
The shells were beads—
things of pleasure and adornment.
The Lord's Brethren knew little
of such things—
stamped and trampled
what they did.
They knew more of money,
and its uses.
Pequot / Narragansett Taught, or tried to,
those better left alone.
And coils of shell heaped up:
What we have called
an Indian exchange.
Small example,
                    but worse to come.
Disease and corruption
high on the list.

(and this sky

sitting perilous
as the wind blows west.
Clouds form in.
Showers in flood time—
a freshet.
                    Interlude.
the afternoon clearing.
Warm enough to sit
by an open door—
a fire beyond,
mixing and changing seasons.

Place to brood
or to rest—
arms akimbo—
head bent - not quite asleep.

Other news:
Scalping, and the bloodthirsty use
of those wars
brought to them
by those same freebooters
who later falsified the texts—
heightening ceremony to commerce.
Always the trade—
value received or given.
It became the measure of friendship.
Use and abuse, synonymous.
All of these things forced
where they could not be foisted
by lies and promises
to be broken as easily
As ice in the spring.
Church-going and deceit—
reverse sides of the same coin.

John Endicott   Their chieftain—hothead, bigot,
one to whom appearances
were important, so long as
they were his alone.
Grim, foul-spoken, even
as he invoked his God,
haunter of courts and jails—
paragon to his blinded peers.
We have yet to go beyond him.
He set the pace—
a stain on everything to follow.
And yet, simply one in a long line
of those before and after.
Our legacy.
A key dropped once in the blood—
and cannot be washed or sanded
free of it.

The native wisdom:
That what became 'up-country'—

the woods and the north mountains—
were for common hunting,
not to be settled.
ignored, of course,
                    and we suffer now
for that ignorance.
As little better than slaves,
the rightful owners—
forced in winter
to follow traplines
for England's furs.
Insatiable greed,
and no costs reckoned.
We must answer,
our children's children pay
for these, and other crimes
against the land.
The state held up, superior,
but the state does fall.
The land returns ill for ill,
-dispassionately-
good for good.
Few know the difference,
and the records sift
precious little but lies and euphemisms.
Set it straight?
Ha!
There are men here.
Only men.

LXXXIV

Twin sparks—
or you alone know what this means—
how we got out of the middle,
not the midpoint.
Small difference, but real,
renewed as poles

which join, but at their ends—
line of axis between them.

Forgetting what it is to forget—
a common heritage—
in common speech—
as this:
What is mine is theirs also.
How do I give of myself
what is already not mine?
And yet mine, as it is theirs—
not theirs?
Flying blind on this one—
enjoying the movement—
freedom.
cold - morning - wood - piled -
lists - forward.
Back and forth (fro)
in and out
or 'filling'
NOTHING STAYS BALANCED.
equal—
              achieves it
in the spin.

The cul de sac
from which these points
appear.
Greater than their substance
for the lack around them.
Chance,
              even as the match
broke in two
                  -two matches-
osage orange   or those trees, chopped in pieces,
to make a hedge of thorns
'so tight, a pig could not force through them.'
Eventually trees once more.

It all takes a working in,
a self-swallowing,
but not the worm's.
Balance will not stay,

returns briefly—
always the chance of it.
Remember the wind,
as remembering is to remember,
enantiotropic:
                    to forget.
How much further out?
They'll come in!
The dawn of a meaning.
(Whatever made is live.
If he who makes it
cannot understand this,
then he is dead—
and what life he might have had
is added to his things.
I don't need to dream
to feel and know that much.

Reflected from the color itself,
anything is mirror.
His face,
as he bent over the red card.
As after the respite,
angers begin again,
in storm and rage
dependant on the source.
No more than that.
Whatever I pick up
depends upon where I am,
and here is where I leave from
live place
              only as I live there.
A fortune spawned on rocks.
Caution, that you speak to them.
There is life,
                    are terrors.
Wind it down again.
What is made is live.
That's it:
Where I pick up and know this—
blindness leaving.
I am whole again.

Where so many things
(other)
have died—
these few.
Arrows of some straight metal
that will not break or warp,
limber / lithe,
strength of their living in them
lie on the floor
                    scattered,
but with a sense of life
in the scattering—
as it prepares to give death—
a further form—
it—
        and not it.
But did I scatter them?
And who was the arrowmaker?
I looked for him,
but there was no one who knew—
or through whom.
Only the arrows which come
                        through—
a clutch—quiver full.
The bow is another question.
Another life.
Only one bow to fit one arrow?
I don't know.
I am asking for help in this,
before the string goes taut,
and the air takes flight—
a burning rise.
Coming in from the raw cold
to whole fires,
heats of some design,
and that pattern at the back of my eyes,
unfocused yet,
glare from the sun still at me.
(Sun?
        but was it sun?
or snow that kept the sun?
that keeps a light
later?

when the sun is gone,
and still the light
which cannot be reflection,
what it stores,
reserves,
pale echo light.
                    Pale. Pale.)
I broke away once,
submission in violence.
I turn these things over.
Kick these arrows
for the sheer pleasure of sound—.

Once more to give orison:
I have risen quickly,
but with no heart in it.
I hardly wanted this cold,
sitting on the chest at the end of the bed,
putting on my socks.
-Some sort of thing like that-
no excitement in it,
simply what I find to do.
A day to find the life in things.
Nowhere to begin,
and no one to help me.

In all such things, the sensors.
I am with them.
I am one of them.
I do not fly so blind
as I once thought.
Next to me, these tools,
and some are living,
all are life.
These many forms
make out my route,
and I must take them,
each in hand.
as arrow, and as bow.
It was a long time ago.
It will be a long time hence.
I am not the only one,
though I am alone

on this road—
this parallel to others.
Bring me in.
Oh, let me come.
The sparks are lit,
just where I dropped them.

LXXXV

Wherever he thinks himself—
he is not.
He is hidden
        and
he is not—.
An island riding out the mist—
a sudden thaw,
          obscured,
and yet observed.
The here and now
           (not now
there.)
He would be private,
but draws attention—
cynosure.
        His secrecy is out.
The men on the mountaintop
cried out
in a loud voice
to the next valley:
'I am! You are not!'
As they thought,
        a joke.
The echo became profound.
Still is
      as it is not—
Wherever it is
         he thinks—
is not—.

Potato Hill
c. 1970

375

Defining the boundaries,
we are set up.
Rocks, tessalated with ice
(pendant)
guards and holds them.
In and out of the country,
easy to find in winter—
elevation in sun,
valleys dark—
rot and wet.
Sun rises over last night's business.
The mountains capped.
A good day promised—
red glare on ice
is
    is not.
Fringe of the day—
that little—
those that fear to go deeper in—.
Crystals that shower the air,
fire and glint.

Wherever he thinks
himself wherever
-thinks or broods-
a piece of it
becoming.
            Far season,
and the sun obscured—
brief shower of snow.

The works of sleep—
some works like sleep,
or words,
            -an ordered context-
sleep at work:
                Its words,
the wards of locks
well-oiled to move,
not slip
            in silence.
How little thinking
have we

in it—
words and works
-the easy ones-
the paving stones—
a storey of them
                under.
Built, and upper.
Hence, I know,
wherever I think
is not,
        or is, of sleep:
his story - generated -
upper sense of it—
the last good sleeping of the night.

And finding it difficult,
he rose out of himself.
He had no sense further,
nor needed it.
His lineage far back,
and worked of what was not—
-no abstract-
into this, and from it,
and the dream made live—
his first
        delight.
All of the affirmative
peeled down
            to echo
in these hills—
to crack the rock
(peel or peal???)
an earthquake seizing them.
Its tremor,
            terrible to feel—
and not know—
                wordless without a wind.
created - well -
half—.
Is and is not
            within.
Precise—the torn envelope
shed of its contents.

Do not forget,
I was caught—he was—
the dream went on
between and around us.
We were frightened,
yet we kept on—
up out of the void.
Hidden in a day,
out a day—
sunlight on the page of lust.
A hidden eye,
and no shade on the window.
It is hard for me to go on,
but I do in spite of that—
heat on the page
found out by the pen's tip wandering.

(Trees in the forest—
                    dead hulks
which no one picks up,
sleeping their heat away
among swamps.
And south
            as the year comes full—
a place for it—
day after day—
warm rot in

I looked for less than I found—
a skyful of birds—
a few skimming the ground
looking for prey—
what is as is not.
A ferment of such decisions—
what there is to pick up.
That which is not hidden,
hides of itself
in the strength of the light.
Is not, as not,
yet is.
A good day.
A good night's sleep.

LXXXVI

Wait a bit—
a bit that we talk
and that we talk about those things
usually hidden—
sometimes that they are hidden
from those who talk—
sometimes swept under the rug.
It is easier *not* to talk of them.
It is easier
        (for)
to forget.   (Death is not forgotten
exactly,
        but fobbed off:
"Wait a while, sir,
I know you're there,
but I have things to attend to.
You won't mind?"
Of course he doesn't.
Comes on anyway.
The stroke is merely one for him
who stays outside the possibilities
and hides.
The man who says:
"Hello, morning,"
          and then looks
at a tide calendar,
thinking in terms of an 'actus tragicus'—
perhaps, literally, that one.
(whistles 'Gottes Zeit' at breakfast.)
Wait!
      The echo (out a window)
nothing waits.
        Still,
if in peace,
        a peaceful standing.
The mourning dove
           -ubiquitous-
association,
      ah,
and now.

Los Angeles,
2/27/76

Any place—
carrying the same sound.
Message is not in it—
as on a curved thorn
hooked into my arm,
wait a bit.
It is a sound of morning.
(Spend the day,
                    later,
in a making—
              gift—
a carved artifact—
scrimshaw or love spoon—
that old man who put his tools
to work each morning
after breakfast,
                    and in silence.
Dependant upon place and time.

The impressions ask for writing—
save them up
in a box
to be sorted later.
Relationships are there.
Find them—the contrasts.
I'll flow on around
or out
not this water.
Nothing leaked.
it is direct force.

Leave that for the moment,
questions rising,
"In the shadow of the sun,
the man himself?"
and where does that fit?
one bit of glass—
sharp prickle under the skin—
question asked—
and asking itself—
turned in on the shadow
that the shadow will not rise.
Is heavy, palpable, shade.

The man in outline—
a chalk drawing of the man,
without the subtleties.
All this cultivated tilt
which makes us
                    less and less.
Eat of the raw things—
water from the spring.
One word brings down complexities
which have no reason
in their being.
Take pleasure in coarse taste.
The man himself
                    an echo.

(In sleep, saying:
"From that which happens,
to that which happens to be."
Could place it somewhere.
The form as intonation.
'Wait! Wait!'
                    Gone again.
Unbearable,
                    or crumbled out,
the renewal into the sea
happens
          (to be.)

The form becomes a license.
What we permit
we find,
          on time,
or out of that.
Somewhere else a mention of it.
Presumed you were there—
a startling overlay—
hard (to be.)

As the time of day opened
and the movement
seen through half light—
those high clouds again:
Altocumulus lenticularis—

Organ Mountains
   3/5/76

lower, a haze, distance—
the home mountains—
                   lodestar.

ibid. 3/6/76

And the sound was broken.
in the next valley
a sound—
          not an echo
nor a distance—
               its own sound
waiting.
At that moment the pot cracked—
flawed beyond use.
Was it the sound?
broken through?
Wait a bit!
Hangs in the air—
its own sound.
I wondered what I was doing there.
In that dry place remembered:
An island in a river
ís an ait.
It was my own helplessness.

I could not live in cities,
so I left.
I do not love the aggregate.
-man in his billions-
causes leave me cold.
But man to man,
a voice to anser
face to face—
wait a bit.
I'll try.
Somewhere in the space and us,
a love is free
to change our breathing,
and to breathe
               itself.
Where I came out to—
from the mountains
and *my*self.

LXXXVII

NY—composite
1976

I have seen them hanging—
gloves in he wind—
or were they
         severed
hands ?
Heads on pikestaves.
Man's inhumanity
-whatever-
         It is something
I have seen.
No matter how little,
I have seen it.
It amuses many.
         It
enters fantasy,
and what they mistake
for love—
         making it
harder to separate.
Organized, it becomes
goodwill—the
         hazing
before one joins.
It is the spark
of much that would
reform us all.
Mistaken spur—
the hatred that enters
in a righteous curse.
An end to that!
There are no causes.
Men do not change
by force,
         or force of rhetoric.
Take us out of it,
but that is magic,
and to work magic
we must believe in it.
Believe, then!
It is as easy to chain wind

with rocks.
(We've done that—
rarely come whole.)
We delight in violence—
stories of it.
Armchair bickerings
over who killed whom.
Heroes with scalps
hung to the waist.
An end to it!
(But I do not see it ending.)
We live easier

The 'Movement'
1955-1970

with natural disaster
than with ourselves.
Some look to a good life
beyond all this,
but invoke old rules
to achieve it.
We have learned nothing!
History? His story.
Close the books.
They are false accounts
at best.
Creeds?
Say the same of them.
Do not invoke peace,

Denise Levertov,
The Freeing of
The Dust

and by the same token
dream of the death
of enemies.
That is no peace.
The old blood flows
in you.
See what you see,
whether it is whole

                        or not.

Know it.

Cesar Vallejo
George Oppen
Keith Wilson

I will listen to those voices
which speak of these things
with authority
-often quiet-
beyond praise or blame.
But the fury of others,

those who know by hearsay,
passes by.
They have no power,
no matter what

The 'resistance'
1965-1972

righteous intonations.
It is not enough
to view from a distance.
Cry an end to it!

Pick up what is around you.
The elements are there
-good and evil-
and by the lights of that place
where you are camped
you will read.
Distance
       blurs the light.

1976

Now a time of wishful thinking,
and the feet stick fast.
Morass and jungle,
heat and disease.
Disappointment—
all of us
       holding on.,
What seemed stone
crumbles.
       Pumice first,
then ash.
It is not a principle
that can save us.
Principles and theories—
economics / politics—
reasons.
These are the pikestaves.

Man to man.
Voices in laughter.
Sorrow.
       A kiss for sign.
The many ways of going.
Doing as each sees best
for himself.
And to groups—

the 'in-crowd.'
To bed at night,
each man in his own environ.
And in the morning
a single sun—
but seen
how various!

LXXXVIII

That pause—
                    space—
silence as I wait
for an elevator
up
     or
          down.
And those around me
silent, too.
A wedge
          heavy in the day.
Only a moment,
but the time around it
splits.
There is always a bridge
back or forward
over it—
a current deep and final
through the day.
The day takes on a color
or a sound—
seeks for the weight
of what has split it.
I am immersed in this,
but feel a separation, too.
That movement,
and its silence.
Coming through, I am not the same man.

Somehow not,
and yet not changed.
I'm opening again,
just as the door opens,
pushes shut
a second later.

It carries across
even now,
back in the context
where the time
brings animal spirits
                    rising.
'Clear this morning
for me—
wind and airs.
You southern ones,
high, higher,
come and sing
this day, this day.'
Or if I had old instruments
to do the saying of it:
A chest of viols,
lute or mandolin,
as part of living,
not the precious ghost of it.
But in this joy
and waking up,
the space-
          that space—
no matter where
behind me.

All of it that goes before,
and did I know it?
Did I see any of it—
chiasma in that space.
It blurs,
          and I am blurred—
only the outline of my hand.
and that is fog.

Then: "The time doesn't always stay one place.
It moves around."

I had it
from a child—who else
could say such things and mean them?
Seriously?
(Just as a cup of tea was steaming cold.)
I'd given thanks,
                    and these
for Olson's last books—
                    and Louis'—
to the end of 'A.')
The time that will not stay—
I shrug and say:
"The craft will survive this—
even this
            much."
And mean it, reverently.
It helps with the space

There are others—
                    pauses—
Clause of condition.
(So *fragile* is the wind,
and yet it does survive us all.)

"For the elements changed their order with one
                                another,
Just as the notes of a psaltery vary the character of
                                the rhythm,
Containing alwas the same, each in its several
                                sound.—"
So one finds whatever
in these old airs
may be of use to him.
And in that use
strikes out the space.
In those desires, a secret,
desires most secret in themselves—
what the love knows, bringing,
or can bring.
A man in his ship of months
before the box of days—
those many-colored stones.
How he will sustain it—
or go from here.

Wisdom: 19, 18

A time in density—
yet with spaces—
hardly spaces him.
'I whirl in fortune,
oh most fragile wind.
The fraction—
                              miniscule—
takes me up.
Put me to sing again."
And I had known myself
in country where I could not know.
A loosening of contradictions—
yet I said no more than that,
and sang old airs,
and learned old maxims.
Was it not the place of heat?
(The colors varied—
were not black or white.
A younger man, I thought them so.
What we do learn
we cannot give another.
It is not bequeathed.
Such as what we have
completes a mystery.)
They had my days,
and on that ship I sailed,
remembering the spaces,
how lacunae came,
even in a trough of waves.
(Lagoon?)
or in the melting of the snow.
I looked outside.
I heard no sound—
but sound was all around me,
even as a fire
built it up.

(A steady leak:
Melt and rain,
thaw and mist—
the days go back
and forth—into themselves—
a fulling of the year.

I look out for my time
and for yours.
It will come—
that steady march—
as the tread of one
greater than any of us.
We have had days together.
We will have more.
The rain goes on.

The space becomes actual.
I see the other side of it—
coming into a mist,
yet leaving at that moment.
The silence is a void.
The pause—
                    the people in it—
not actual.
Day alone is palpable.
I have entered that day.
In the end:
All that matters—
that we do not matter—
(end.)

LXXXIX

Evening—as an
EVENING out—
stretching to the bounds—
the light in chains.
I come across it—
stray light on lock of hair,
(these straying)
this table,
              its papers shadowed.
Will it hold?
long enough?

or will I come back to it?
going out the door.
Flattened this side,
as the sun raises
                and rises
another
          side a side of
being.

It was hard enough to arrange these things—
this furniture—
before the light changed it all—
nothing more or less
than the half hour before darkness.
Wind—a long way from the sea—
but slight sea breeze,
stirring only a few branches,
restless. One after another.
An evening of temperaments—
not colors.
She said we shouldn't view the full moon
through a window.
Outside then,
but that's for later.
We will move there in another hour.
For now it is enough
to take TWIlight
sunSET.
It is hardly this place longer
than it has been.
Such light is strange,
even as it is one of those common
well-loved things
from each day.

The quiet authority I feel
waiting for someone
not knowing what
he may be going through to get here.
I am impatient for it,
almost, but not quite, in limbo—
evening.
It is daylight, still

for the man coming to me
from the other side of the mountain.
Hold this light
that he and I may see each other
before it is dark
or moonlight,
and we come together
by another way / reflection.
It is not easy to clarify
after the fact.
This fact is light
fading into itself—
that its colors strengthen
and do not die out
before they are held.
That moment, just before a death,
when life asserts itself—
the last strong pulse.
This light is that
coming up—
emerald or sapphire—
that the eyes open fully
to receive it.
I am sitting here
inside
and by a window.
Shall I open it?
Or is that for later?
for the moon?
Hard to pick it up.
not a spike or board—
that tangible.
But we touch.

As if the bow were
above the strings—
that sound—
a light so gentle,
(but hard enough to know)
It washes in
at the window—
leaks over these papers—
glances up at me—

pitying sustenance.
It will hold on.
Strike
        for the dark, it
strikes once more.
It comes easily enough,
goes out through the last crystals.
I have given enough play to it.
Myself at this point—
the levels reached—
an evening—
perhaps itself—
the magic and the magician.
It will not stay.
Quickly drops.
Last fires in the trees.
at sea, the rout,
scald of waves.
I am caught once more—
a bone in the teeth.
Evening as evening,
and myself,
a face in the dark.

XC

Midriff:
        MID RIFF-
a diaphragm—
where that takes off
to.
    Fully the refrain—
or the unthought act
of the child, running
finally to all.
What forms on his word.
Sounding—a diaphragm.
Deep pedal tone.

Consideration of the word,
and how the senses slipped.
Always downwards.
Gravity, I suppose.
Pick it up!
These words and places
to ward off—
possibilities linked
                or
otherwise chained.
How one learns of words
that they are not
what they mean—
simply themselves in all their parts.
A difficult route—
around - in back.
The place to touch them—
dim as the mirror in flux—
still, the self,
not the mirror.

Look at this morning
to which I have come.
Here, at the midpoint,
hard as it may be
to come from sleep.
Each day harder,
an illness—
life galled at one point—
the many points—
a howe/barrow:
Ship's burial.

Still—there was this place.
And the place meant
as the words concerning it
did not.
I had come from these readings,
signs of crossed arrows
and firesticks.
Said much about it, and them,
but these were not the words,
and the exactness failed.

I looked for other things:
Failed too.
I planted a stave
but its roots were rotten—
and not of it.
The hard bone of the word.
Later, I picked it up.
That made fortune.

I planted a stone.
Its roots were sand.
It vanished,
and I was left with my pains—
what else?
The words are few,
and they are neither stave nor stone.

What else I planted
came of water,
and its roots were water.
I was alone with it—
nothing counted.
I lost the word in counting.

Cape Cod,
1946-1961

I came up from a valley.
Living there it had seemed
solid—even a good place.
I hear now
that the widows entertain
each other.
But they do not know the words,
or how the words are shaped
in themselves.
They must not be held
or used.
         Conveyance.
Midriff or term.
Stream.
         What are these things?
Other than definition,
a specie,
something of value in itself.
Debased. (Of course.)

395

(Plain chant of a tree.
One note
            as it fell.

The *art* of a word to make this dust—
a hollow out of its own vapor.
At the best it may reduce,
and in degree
                corrode and rust.
Old hinges, brittle,
doors sagging,
                and the house empty.
But there is the chance.
Take it
        by all means.
And in the sound the
            center
dropped.
Later, I found the other half.
This I say of it:
Rises.
        Of some size larger.
Slaps its tail like a fish.
Displaces water
                below.

Schlüssstuck—
a piece of fate
made of itself.
Look at the word.
Savor   sound.

In all these mornings
find the place
            meant,
and do not say it in words
unless the words cohere
as hard as ledge.
                Immoveable.
Marlin spike.
                Belaying pins.
Rope and piton.
                Grab hold.

Make certain.
It is the climb over and out.
This is the only way to brew
a drink bitter enough
to purge the guts.
Black drink of the Creeks
for all our language.
Concision,
                but concision
is not all of it.
One man wills what he will do,
and bounds it.
Another doesn't know.
In either lies the falsehood,
or the honesty.
Can you take me outside these bounds?
Do it.
But if it is in words,
find their country,
not about it.

At one point
what is the separation?
Tools from work?
It would be hard to make it.
Accept the rock for rock,
don't strike against it.
Can we reach through?
There is water so clear
that depths deceive.
What we read there
is at distance.
Only the lens brings the news close.
It has been a long way in.
It is not equal—
the way out.
Guide and malice become description.
There are no guideposts.
We work around—
through strange places.
Always the attempt to see
beyond physical limits
not finite—

the limits of seeing itself.
Perhaps the words in situ
pose these problems.
On a clear day
these things seem easier to access,
but at the first clouds
the positive becomes a whimper.
'I am' is pointless.
No one is able to find a way out.
Quandary deepens.
Well, it may be that the stone guest
does appear,
and reverses the invitation.
Is it the part of a man
to accept?
Can't sidestep it.
Direct defiance is a way,
and also ignorance.

If I had the firesticks!
The power to burn buildings
with a few strokes.
The words turn in on themselves.
I do.
A portion of the way—
only a portion.
I am left with these stones.
A few of them are words.
Feel the weight.

XCI

There is a sad ness:
If love outlasts its people,
subject to itself—
an aimless charge
wandering—
               stray lightning
in a fitful landscape.

I would not believe it,
though it is the experience of some.
A sadness.
?The heavy air before a summer storm :
that kindness curdles,
                              sours ;
gentleness shatters,
brittle to an edge.
A faintness stirs.
Half light.
Color of bronze
                    tarnished.
Set in sadness.

The photograph of an old man
left in the sun too long
blurs and fades
to an outline.
Only the breath remains,
feeble as the pulse—
an aroma.
The ghost of old flowers.
Old loves.

If it is quick ? short-lived ?
A mist between hills ?
In and out ?
A scorching wind both sides ?
Then a dream
is interlude between deaths,
and it may be so.
A lonely world.
These stones wear the boots out.
I am not convinced of it,
though I have seen examples,
and felt them.
These stones wear the heart out.

What is it like ?
to have gone past it ?
to have left home,
and gone the other side of the mountain ?
Is it frailty ?

or blindness to the world as it is?
Sometimes I think so.
Often I envy those old men
who drink nothing but cold water,
contemplate the stars
and the sun—
                    all seasons the same.
But I cannot follow them.
These risks cut to my bones.
I may outlast them.
But love will go beyond me.
Elusive at its best.
It will complete a circle,
as I will my own.

Rage, it is true, has something to do with it—
rage, and spent rage.
Rage, in its time, foretells and dismisses.
The hand passes its fire—
crippled or purified—
neither right nor left.
Where is the language for it?
What are its uses?
Day lowers again
-its clouds-
                    a chance of rain.
and the rain may pass by;
a few drops, unstable,
trembling in the wind.
Ash pale - ash pale.
Only a love that burns
escapes compromise.
The burning consumes it.
There is fuel, always,
but the fuel runs low.
Replenish it?
Find source.
Comfort no object,
the men now no longer crave wealth.
They look for power—
how they may injure other men.
That is their source—
blind to any other.

Wells in dry country,
they have chosen the bitter one.
It is not early enough for dew.
Parches the throat.
The desert marches.

There is a thorn bush ,
cuts and recurves its claws
in torn clothing and flesh.
Firethorn, acaccia,
mesquite, and the crown, in its mats,
crucifixion thorn.
We all walk there.
It is hard to come out of that land
without blood—
                shed and neglected.
The ground takes its share.
No key—no formula.
It is best to leave the maps at home.
The intersect of trail and grid
confuse.
Known patterns frighten off.
Hindsight. Let us have that—
not a prophecy.
Little we'd do
if we knew all the dangers
in a drawn breath.
The pleasures?
Ah, there are many.
And the cactus blooms briefly,
in the spring,
whenever there is rain enough.
(The day still lowering—
no rain.)
We look for something new.
His story repeats itself.
Are there no new things?
Why do we look for them?
Colors in the spectrum recombine:
The same colors.
Knowledge and the news
cannot wear out.
But we rarely look at them to know it.

The mists blow warm,
pass,
        and the edges sharpen.
(But the edges cut as keen,
no matter what the mists.)
A pavement in the sky—
few spits of snow.
The rain passed over—
destroying angel:
not yet—not yet.

The end of all these things
is hazzard.
Seed compensates.
One man becomes another.
-several- -any-
When we follow him,
we follow after,
                and ourselves.
What quickness in the light.
I'd not forgotten—
death—or any of the rest of it.
Sounds solid.
                Is antique.
Could we suffer
so to change it?
so to rise out of it?
Sadness is not heavy.
Cards are stacked.
They chance it.
Love is worth the change.

XCII

Pools of water on old ice.
Then it must be spring—
a tide in the rising.
The raw edge of the earth
its selvage / hem

ripped out and made again.
In what small ways
we find the news—
the levers which have moved
the mountains—split the rocks—
or cut the furrows
in an old man's face.
It's all the same.
(The skin on the backs of my hands
lies loose and wrinkled now.
Each year I find it more so.
*In*to things the seep of water—
grain of rust.
I've turned it over in my bed—
the bed for water,
fleck or flash—
gold and pyrite in solution.
No matter where it goes.
The season follows—
dogged in its flow—
the down down down
of movement.
(And the wind on water.
Pools on ice.)

And this will last
until the colors change

                              no more:
The blue-green to its yellow—
the darker to the blaze
which is autumn's answer.
How, in that dust,
the pools and the ice
are caught napping

                         implicit.
An old man—
his sleep after lunch.
When will that sleep—?
better not ask that question.
We'll be coming in
to it

        once more.

And the breeze bears chill
from the high mountains.
No matter the sun.

Waxes oracular.
How do I talk?
only of those things
I remember from a long time ago?
Sort through the impressions
of the moment!
Each moment the surrogate
To his own the answers,
if the answer serves him.
I see no way beyond.
Best not to divide.
Layer on layer,
let them speak
in their own stress.
Well, there is a time
for it.
The old man still has
something to say.
It is not all mumbling.
The young man mumbles
until he puts pebbles
in his mouth,
(loses breath to find it)
He can do this
in his own time.

The trouble with spring is
that it runs out
like sand—
but only to the receptor—
if he will not receive.
And the melting
can loosen old cheek furrows,
as it does a ploughed field.
When were we young?
When will we turn young again?
There is nothing in life
like the question.
The answer has no worth
                 comparable.

They left shards here,
or sticks to burn—
some caught in the rock—
sedimentary made hard.
The old bones are new bones,
Take up the passage.
The vein of any man
conveys to his heart.
A lust in the eye—
better,

        say lustre.
Glint of the pool.
The sediment

           settles
only for a time.
The freshets break it up
again and again.

Bring me a bucket—
I need something to sweep away water.
The pools lie only in daylight.
Skim ice by dark—
and at midnight—

             hard slick—
treacherous.
Old men who winter it
will die in the spring.
Fatten the land—
their blood will warm it.
The ice goes out slowly.
I dip my hand
in its water.

XCIII

Possibly true:
That
       all a man has thought
would go on a half sheet of paper—

E.P. from Hulme
Guide to Kulchur

the rest being what he thought *about* it,
But there are wings to pick it up,
places to go from what he thought
to where.
I'm interested in places.
If I could not take time in trips—
two or more each year,
I would feel deprived.
How much more inside a man!
And there is that in essence
is not palatable
nor understood,
                    can spread
by some thinkings further,
into what may nourish.
Liking myself,
                    I'll take off from there,
and go on saying what I like.
Like today:
I'm going swimming again
-the first time for the season—
but having done it once
does not reduce it.
'It takes doing again'.'
Getting at,
if that's a way of saying it.
Read the old books,
play the old music.
Keep an eye and an ear open.
The limitations do not limit.
Thank you.

In our own time,
we've got the convention down pat,
and not much more,
even if it's 'each his own' conventions.
Take off from that.
It needs more.
By sleight you can say
that these are all there are—
but it is
          sleight / slight.

I want the whole of the man.
Anything said
            made absolute
withers to the bone.
And there's where we have little of it.
To simplify sometimes extends.
That much of material
                    process.
Fully cooked?
            Ha!

One day it sets on edge,
the next, a full agreement.
The urge to say
                anything,
anything not needed—
upsurge—
            let it have its say.
Today
      assayed.
A whole life in its passage.
I drop something
into a shirt pocket:
Bottom's out—
                lost - lost.
Couldn't believe this life.
I've spent too much on it.
Paces exactly,
(and what I reject, being given it,
is the cornerstone more times
than I would want to build from it.)
Working through a maze—
turning back again.
Early in the morning so
                    still - still.
Doublings and turnings.
We will do little
dropping the apoggiaturas.
There are those who feed
on what is there—
snails and roots at the bottom.
To analyze,
find out the water,

other percentage—
doesn't stop them—
nor what will nourish.
Oh these people.
Their exactness.

Digesting it:
Do we want the acorn, or the oak?
Even a dry branch
to break—
                    start a fire
on a cold night?
And from the cold,
what then?
I measure time.
so. much. time.
I will not stop
at essence or elixir.
Tensing a hand—
flexing a muscle
                    once?
Compare these things.
Whatever they are,
we take what we have
into the seasons around us.
And they are changed—
as the seasons change with them.
There is music—
                    much of it—
and I want that music
more than the elements
flat and uncontroverted.
Not to set it up—
that is fiction—
breaks through credence.
Do not do it!
A way in and out again.
A man—
                    all of him—
passes through.
Beware of the simple statement.
It does not
hold water.

A manifesto in the *whole* history—
clarity there.
Only when the water
settles
      out
its mud / detritus.

It is not that there is
so much
      here
or there—
      or that we
(I) should listen
to the end of each tautology.
But the flesh is needed,
and the bone
      -though beautiful-
is not the sum of beauty.
Clever statements—
and knuckles should be rapped.
Whatever the mastery,
it is not in thinking.
The sum which makes
rules it out.
(Come to it later.
Possible.)

A snatch of this music—
far out—
heard at large.
It *is* large.
How to say this well?
No, how to say it.
Take no thought to it,
blinders maybe,
escape the finish / trap.
All of this—
      this music.
Haydn, at the moment,
yes, could be boiled down
to a single note,
but I prefer the length of it.
Opening the window

onto a whole world—
not a distillate—
pale and unchanging.
Elements of those who lie
by day in coffins—
walk only at night
to feed on living.
It is not the legend that keeps them
quick.
It is alive,
and there are motionings
down - around them.
They rise,
            slowly,
nature as an old moon
at old ways.
It is a hard thing to know:
To take a man—
a woman—
bride in her honesty—
as the unfaithfulness
sure to follow.
And still - it is to take—
whole.
The only way of it.

(Is the raga
            repeated?
useless and unnecessary?
Marshal your thought elsewhere.
I say—dismissal.)

That half sheet of paper, then,
runs on
until another life
                surely
and cleverly
            cuts it.

XCIV

White against white
                    (green)
(red)
        blaze of it—
take it all—at all seasons.
To steal a thousand ways
for it—
          the bases—
simply another way
to look through a window.
Whatever is there
is not what comes back
as the sight—
the mirror—my eye.
I could hardly say this
without reflection—
                    the mind's
sight.
Before. I must have been there
before.
But what is it I'm saying?
I am doing a little
in and out.
My bones—?
Forget the bones.
It is fluid
          any light.

(I am treading bottom here,
but not to trust—
the current comes on—
winter flood—
spring freshet.)

Never a clean page.
It is all set here—
a danger to go on.
to go back—?
more danger.
White against white.
Shake out the leaves

degree on
        degree,
and as they color,
touch the page with them.
A day by the window,
or a year—
simply a glance through it.
Nothing touches.
the mesh comes apart in the wind,
goes together
        in the wind
again.
An energy—
        high delight—
It will hold
even as the grip
drops.

Where have we been?
Thickness of head—
shake, old pollard,
dreams.

Then a skein of sound,
to carry / pass through.
The dull day
becomes brighter.
The colors hold—
burn in their heat—
slowly—as a shimmer.
Walking inside the sound,
it is not shade—
yet shields.
It makes easily.
The thickness gives way
to the sharpness of dreams.
There is that place,
stance
        near the window—
not looking out, necessarily,
where everything is possible.
The ripeness.
        The love.

"Do as thou wilt."
It comes—leaves—
an odd tone
            intoned.
Out, but rightly out.
Night does not obscure it.
This light—
skein of sound.
A script, set in—
lichen or mold.
It rains often
beyond this window—
and the pivot of rain
presses in.
Unbearable mornings—
evenings after aimlessness—
sleep like a stone—
with no reason for sleep—
nothing to recoup.
Will broken—
the leached stalks of another year
under the rain.
My window—
my colors seen against
others.

Come back!
And I turn away.
There are things to do
-a way of doing them-
out of inanition.
A focus.
"Denke an Deine Sicherheit."
Where does that come?
Oh well,
safety in focus—
out of the wind—
lying in deep grass.
The rain is over.
Colors, only as the clouds
lie
      high in color—
white on white

on blue, on all the eye projects.
Not there.
It is never there.
But here it is.
Glass shattered from my window.
First tensed and flexed.
But we see brittley,
and think so is not so.
                    (Sehnsucht / Sicherheit—ha!
Better words in German.)
Listening to voices—
always the sounds of children.
They have no echo.
Whispers. (Listen
The color purifies
the day in rising
out
      and topmost.
Spar for pleasure—
catching a stream
to hold the current.
Cannot always stay at windows.
Why a window?
                    Place broken open:
a breach.
(Lets in as much light—
a jagged frame.)
It comes foremost,
another morning.
The words come like the mists—
their balance in themselves.
Not what they mean.
How could they?
                    (eh?)
Time as the temper.
All my time
gives color.

XCV

Death is a partner—
lightens the going.
There is no burden—
dust, impalpable,
the comet's haze.
Ahead.
       This surety.
Talking evenly—this death.
No fear in it.
Take what is known as nothing.
It is unknown,
only agreed upon,
and there comes death again.
A portion of the will—
the force leaps up to it.
It would contend,
but there is nothing there
to touch.
The senses slip by—
a mist of cold—
obdurate darkness—
neither light nor shade.
Conscious of it,
slow - spiral - turn.
This is the usual way.
There is another.
In those levels
rarely entered,
it is easier, and the senses
catch on fire.
Not by difficulties.
We are not known or remembered
by them, except as catchwords.
Move over, this must have its say.
It is the death of it
that reimburses.
Ascent to the hill—
each chance, if you will make it so.
Where does the wheel stop?
Or the wind?

It is not a stopping place.
Reach down and find it.
Clench of the fist—
the will to die
is in the living—
a long stop
in the spring, lighted
by airs and turnings.
Acceptance comes,
                    this quiet
rises.
I am so dead
I must still live.
A simple ditch to siphon water,
stretched across the road—
an accurate design.
Here they are again—
words smeared over everything.
Their future, or ours,
cut - dead.
But this is only for the words.
Other things rise out of them.
Such a tension
beginning the movement.
Or issued,
                cleansed.
The morning makes it—
the afternoon—
                    shadows
from a long stick.
Whatever it was, first,
no longer here.
But the surety—
                    inalienable deed—
a share in it—
and that is for death.
Whatever else has been,
this is a sure case.
No advocates.
Think of it every day—
be with it, or not,
(the against / quarrel

turns into affirmation.
It is hard to go on thinking,
and it is not wisdom
for all the wisdom in it.
Alive, we are most dead,
turned to that place
where death becomes living.
An only friend.
Seal that friendship!
Who will come?
I am /
            / you are.
The make of our being
is no wraith.
Take everything, or
a few pebbles.
The sand is death's property.
Next and pursuant,
these simple things.
We think of their endings,
and forget them.
In later years,
pick them up,
mourn the loss
of what comes between.
Could the tightening occur?
without impatience?
It might, and I might.
centering in wind,
going any direction—
not to for get a partner,
or a parting / together.

XCVI

This grease turns water—
and the water flows away—
whole.
Or take this:
"Too early, the fruit tastes of the tree—
too late,
        of the ground."
All day, the rain.
              Now it clears
again.
)and so some drag or leap
to the sound of it.
It is the open field.)
Once more, a festival,
if it is by season.
Opposites do attract
grease and water.
They do not mingle.
The tree—the ground.
Tensions.

Ah let it be, as it will
be in being.
Interjection then—
the edge on edge—
point to point.
Too simple to resolve this.
What stands out,
             does,
The rest fades,
           a formal mass.
(Law of perspective.)

Question it!
The acceptance of whole meat
upsets digestion.
It *might* be in another form.
Critical waste—
what is approved—
what isn't.
           No questions.

A man dies out in the process—
color of leaves leached—
No questions.
A fortune in this mud,
but who presses it?
A scattering, oh these bones.
Let it be—
            learn to let—
the question.
Whatever I touch
touches back.
Could hardly stand more
or other.
(Thinking here—break off.
            ##############
Censers—
the smell of smoke—
the air is open—
raw and bare.
Carry. Such vehicle.
Well, it's all of a piece,
but the pieces pick up
small
            sense for censer.
Question comes—
                  slips past—
who questions?
Or is the question a lump—
area or not?
Whatever worried me—
a short space—
a time
        shorting
censer
        smoke of the wind
trailing—so easy it must be—
up or over.
Taking time for this, may I
my timing
            break?
It cannot be.
            It is the whisper
fated.

Time's taken, and a man's cold
in the outside.
What attracts / distracts.
And that makes the outside of it.

I could have thought of that!
(But you didn't.
small difference, I agree,
but you didn't.)
The sound steps around the sound,
not around itself.
There is a way of hearing this—
The knot, as it is drawn out,
tightens.
There is no sympathy—
nothing to hold on to as comfort.
simply the knot.
And the knot is against me—
a congener for evil.
Or is it nothing?
How have I spent this morning?
In breaking stones,
as they are breaking me.
In some way I have fought it,
broken over all of it,
and yet I am still here.
The only place for me,
where the winters darken,
the elements separate.
I have known much of this,
year in and out.
All of the divisions—
these oils and waters,
esters and mercaptans.
It is hardly my day yet—
nothing to hold to—
the knot tightens,
and the knot hurts—
a primal wound.
          #############
Look!
I want to work,
and I want quiet to do it in—

but there is rarely that chance.
what we think we have—
that place, separate from other places,
is fouled from the outside.
It does not mix:
Oil and salt and water—
false heterodyne
which we hear and hear and hear.
It comes in again,
and it is brought in.
The bearers of it never learn
                              any thing.
Rationale occurs:
"Just this once won't matter."
"Where's your sense of humor?"
And the words continue to disrupt.
Very well, I'll fix you here,
all of you, your noise and your
disruption.
But it is a far cry from what I wanted,
and the purity doesn't count.
Cry fades off—
                 distance—
the other side
                 (side
the other—.

As if it were easy to set down—
the speed has nothing to do with it—
it is a far cry,
                 and a false one.
(Sometimes a little anger
to pry it loose—
and quiet in the morning—
sounds from birds,
but do they count?

The whole of the day
—that generalized—
and taken up on.
I could be going out—
I hardly sense it as a going.
Dream, and dream worlds

421

coalesce.
All in the words I like
and mark the best—
comes time to turn it over.
I had a fix on it.
Beam shored in place,
and then released.
I went more surely.
(Sounds—
what are the birds about?
staking out a country,
as the rest of us?
Grease in water?
ah! A little of it.
Something keeps it all:
A place where it does not
run off.

XCVII

The land, now,—
its dreaming—
how to remove to it
without removing it.
Silence is dead
                silence,
and the echoes do not come.
Dust, although the sea
surround and girdles it—
small land.
Oh, fragile.
Upland, where the woods have been,
a view—
no woods.

"—This lande laye stretching itself to the West, which after wee founde
to be but an Island of twentie leagues long, and not above six miles broade.
Under the banke or hill, whereon we stoode, we behelde the vallies replenished with goodly Cedar trees,

and having discharged our harquebushot, such a flocke of Cranes (the most part white) arose under us, with such a cry redoubled by many Ecchoes, as if an armie of men had showted all together."

> And was it like—?
> what could we know?
> What did they?
> The cranes have left,
> and the cedars rotted.
> The right of plunder,
> as its rite,
> descended now to motes.
> The light, sure, the light—
> much the same,
> and strength approximate.
> But even that has gone—
> some ten minutes from a day.
> In a year, that much darkness.
> A year of darkness to come on.
> Sounds the same.
> Da Capo, al fine,
> only the finish may be soon.
> The backlands catch it.
> The front crumbled long ago.

—"The first that appeared unto us, we entred, though not without some difficulties, and cast anker about three harquebushot within the havens mouth, on the left hand of the same: and after thanks given to God four our safe arrival thither, we manned our boats, and went to viewe the lande next adjoyning, and to 'take possession of the same in the right of the Queenes most excellent Majestie, as rightfull Queene, and Princesse of the same, and after delivered the same over to your use, according to her majesties grant, and letters patents, under her Highnes great Seale. Which being performed, according to the ceremonies used in such enterprises, wee viewed the lande about us,—"

> So I might ride into New York tomorrow—
> take it, by my own privy seal.
> Madness?
> No worse than this as done
> "according to the ceremonies used
> in such enterprises."
> Time and time again.
> (Columbus tripped and kissed the earth.)

423

"—The 13 we landed on an Iland called Mona, whereon were 10 or 12 houses inhabited of the Spaniards; these we burned & tooke from them a Pinesse, which they had drawen a ground and sunke, and carried all her sayles, mastes, and rudders into the woods, because we should not take them away; we also chased the Spaniards over all the Iland, but they hid them in caves, hollow rocks, and bushes, so that we could not find them.—"

Complete, with the irons for branding:
Slaves, and that concept.
Arrogant, and proud of their 'rights.'
Arrogance begets it—
and twenty generations later,
the same blood flows.

Whose portion is scanted?
Whose denied?
At this remove it makes no difference.
Blood still nourishes cabbage—
whose blood?
Who is to eat it?
Massacre, and mob law—
lynching, torture.
The western tour digs one long grave.
Split skulls
for coyote and vulture.
If we leave the pack,
we are pursued,
hunted down.
Most recant.
The road to conversion
lies through dungeons:
Gehenna and Sheol.
We have learned nothing.
Point up the history with pride.
(Point it, but do not read it.)
The simplest things forgotten—
'a lost art.'
Who grows apples anymore?
unless they shore the growing
with technologies and poison?
Leaving nothing,
careen from side to side—
carom shot—

lurching through a tunnel
to one patch of light.
The mountain all above them,
and the sun.
This is the way on:
                        To Conquest!
"Fight it!"
watchword for everything—
from disease to Nature—
back again.
All fights are one.
I do not live here easily.
The days dry up
in their own brine—
savorless salt.

Taking to flight from it—
there is no flight,
and conscience the worst of congeners.
Remorse or rage,
what does any of it bring?
More remorse.
More rage.
There is a chorus—
something sounding from all sides—
every instrument into it.
It is precarious ground—
deadfalls and traps
mine it.
A firm grip—no grip—
and the armor is rusted.
Grim happiness,
if there is such a thing.
The land is dreaming.
Goes on dreaming.
It supports the fault and the ache.
"Machet die Tore weit
und die Türen in der Welt hoch—"
That who may come?
Who comes into these silences?
Grieving, step aside.

XCVIII

Bent,
     as a cane is bent,
an old man leaning—
into the wind.

Climbing, above shelter,
he came to a place where the mountains
held their ranks—
north and south.
          A backbone.
He watched the sunrise,
turned his shoiulder and
             saw it set.
Should he go east?
or go west?
Should he catch the light
as it came up, dripping,
            from one sea,
or dive into another to watch it quench?
The light to the east seemed pure.
The west brought dust and sweat.
(Those who went west
           brought wars
and destruction.
          Those to the east
sought to be alone
          or in peace.
The same spot moves, either way,
dependent upon how the look is persuaded.)

With him, the man brought spiders,
small ones in the pages of a book.
If one is killed
it will rain.

"What will you give me—
back for song?
or what is song but blood?
I shed and I do not
shed."
          Bite the lips:

Diane di Prima

Salt and songs
come in a rush—
the same heat—
                    the same source—
the same
            the same
same
        same
                same
ticking.
(The pacemaker
bent on *his* cane.)

(sings again)

"That space—
that very space and air
holds us for ourselves,
but is not empty.
Silence sits at midnight
on the stairs—
a restless silence
in that space."

Again.

"What about them?'

Of will and spirit,
only the spirit remains.
Faint incense—
                    naphtha—
mothballs in a closed chest.
Here and there,
                    look it over.
(Old man bent
            over his treasure.)
Little to find.
The will, uncorked like wine,
will breathe at first,
then go flat.
Here and there.
Look.
It *is* over,

and the fires are out.
A young man tried it.
He essays.

        Then what?
The spirit protects itself.
Shrouds and hides.
It remains.
A fall haze over the mountains.
So fragile—

        rise into it.
(Hortatory or not—
the bent stick and the bent back.)
So, if you will,
try it out—look for
the directions.
These are the cautions—
we come close
and curious.
Oh, hold on, a minute.
Give time.
(Breathless in this country
and much sweat.
So, propped

        over he went.
He fell

    down.)
And the down is trying.
Rise / rise
ARISE
over the first rise.
The sun's in its heat.
The will is either way.
We have sensed much more,
but we've lost—
what was it?
A horse? A leaf? An echo?
Push on to the sunrise.
Come on it in the sea.
Gulled into it—
it is nostalgia,
but it can go further—
over and

        out.

Scope and size, releasing,
I must convince them.
Converging, we will,
together.
            That man's sun
is all men's.
But all stand at differing angles.
Warmth in the hollows,
cold shadows behind them.
Blood tracks in the snow,
but is it blood,
or the sun's doing?
Another doing—
                yet another.
Day after day—the high pure air,
even the storms cannot erase it.
The man strides.
His cane is a prop,
or in case of need.
He sheds his age.
Exults.
            He hardly comes down—
the plains through which he passes
are high as the peaks behind him.
Escarpment of the land.
No land, and no maps.
The festivals are in the sun.
It is between the man and the sun,
and the earth has vanished.
Feet touch light.
Its substance sustains.
Let him exult, then!

It is closer than the stars,
years of light that stood between
are gone.
"Ghostly and alone."
He can say it aloud.
His answer is in himself.
No need.
            No needs.
He sheds his clothes.
Here he is again!

He drops his cane.
A dry clatter somewhere below.
Ice or rocks receive it.

It is dark around him.
The light of the sun holds itself:
Only for the sun.
No matter. He has enough in himself,
for warmth and light.
Ghosts or wraiths.
Sound is separate—
in itself—no hearing.
Bent, but the bend is the curve of space.
Age has no meaning.
Nothing but the curve,
and down.
No, the directions vanish.
Pull of all attractions.
Nothing remains but the sun.
Behind the sun, a sea.
Not the one he sought.
He goes in
-out or around-.
In the sea.
Life was sweet.
And this sweet death.

End of Book 3   June 1975—June 1976